ASSOCIATION MANAGEMENT EXCELLENCE

Become an Expert By Preparing for the CAE Exam

D.A. ABRAMS

D.A. ABRAMS

Copyright © 2014 D.A. Abrams
Second Edition © 2015 D.A. Abrams
Ingram Spark Edition © 2019 D.A. Abrams

All Rights Reserved
ISBN: 978-1-7334-3133-0

Association Management Excellence

AUTHOR'S NOTE

This book is the second edition of my manual, *Certified Association Executive Exam: Strategies for Study & Success*, published in 2013. It includes thirty percent new material, including condensed summaries of my books *New-School Leadership: Making a Difference in the Twenty-first Century* and *Diversity & Inclusion: The Big Six Formula for Success*.

Many readers of this book's first edition have shared with me the various positive ways that using this as a guide to prepare for the CAE Exam has directly enhanced their overall Association Management skills. They appreciated the experience and benefited personally and professionally whether they sat for the formal exam or not.

I dedicate this new edition to your own professional development as a CAE, and hope you, too, will share your feedback and study experiences after you read and work through the material.

INTRODUCTION

There are over 92,000 trade, membership, and professional associations in the United States, and more than one and a half million charitable or philanthropic organizations, each managed by Association executives and professionals who are dedicated to the mission, services, and social good provided by their institution. Perhaps you are one of these executives. Or maybe you are considering a career in this important field. You may be surprised to learn that there are, in fact, only 4,000 Certified Association Executives, a mere 2.5% of all professionals managing associations and non-profit organizations. The CAE certificate is one of the most selective and unique credentials in business today.

I had been an executive with the United States Tennis Association for eighteen years when I undertook my own preparation for the CAE certification. My ambition was not just to obtain the prestige and distinction of the credential. Nor was I influenced too much by the fact that it would support my imminent promotion to head of diversity and inclusion at the USTA. Primarily I sought the recognition of my skills, experience, and capabilities as a senior association executive, and a confirmation of my understanding of the best practices for managing an organization at a top level.

My process of preparing for the CAE examination and for meeting the application requirements was somewhat self-taught. I did participate in one of the American Society for Association Executives' immersion study courses that are held twice each year in Washington, D.C., and found it to be helpful. But I recognized that a great deal of additional information could serve the community of executives that aspire to take this exam every year, and that not all qualified applicants could travel and stay in

Washington, D.C. for three days in order to prepare in that fashion.

This book is designed to do three things. First, it seeks to explain the CAE certification and its many benefits, in the hopes that you will join me in preparing for and attaining this credential. Second, it will provide a step-by-step process for preparing for the CAE examination, strategically and comprehensively. Third, it sets out to explain how to ready yourself for the test itself, and to offer specific recommendations and solid tactics for approaching it, so that you achieve your objective and complete it, successfully and with ease.

My professional work and lifelong commitment to Diversity and Inclusion are integral to my personal understanding of how best to manage and understand non-profit institutional excellence. It is likely that D&I will come to play an enhanced role in the CAE exam, as well, starting in 2015. This book includes an expanded section on D&I that will benefit every executive preparing to take this test and in managing their Associations.

I recently published a book about new-school leadership in the 21st century that details in depth my framework for succeeding as a leader in a dynamic but ever-changing management landscape. As a bonus to my fellow Association Executives who are working through this program to prepare for their exam, I include a chapter that summarizes my book and its key concepts as they may apply in your professional leadership capacity.

Okay, let's begin!

Association Management Excellence

TABLE OF CONTENTS

AUTHOR'S NOTE iii

INTRODUCTION v

CHAPTER 1: WHAT IS THE CAE? 1

    CAE Benefits 4

    Prerequisites for the CAE 6

CHAPTER 2: THE CAE EXAM—AN OVERVIEW 10

    Preparing for the CAE Exam 12

CHAPTER 3: CAE TEST DOMAINS 19

CHAPTER 4: DOMAIN 1—ORGANIZATIONAL MANAGEMENT 22

CHAPTER 5: DOMAIN 2—LEADERSHIP 47

CHAPTER 6: DOMAIN 3—ADMINISTRATION 59

CHAPTER 7: DOMAIN 4—KNOWLEDGE MANAGEMENT & RESEARCH 85

CHAPTER 8: DOMAIN 5—GOVERNANCE AND STRUCTURE _____ 96

CHAPTER 9: DOMAIN 6—PUBLIC POLICY, GOVERNMENT RELATIONS, AND COALITION BUILDING _____ 113

CHAPTER 10: DOMAIN 7—MEMBERSHIP DEVELOPMENT _____ 127

CHAPTER 11: DOMAIN 8: PROGRAMS, PRODUCTS, AND SERVICES _____ 142

CHAPTER 12: DOMAIN 9—MARKETING, PUBLIC RELATIONS, AND COMMUNICATIONS _____ 163

CHAPTER 13: DIVERSITY & INCLUSION—THE BIG SIX STRATEGIES FOR SUCCESS _____ 184

    THE NEW NORMAL _____ 185

    STRATEGY 1: TALENT OPTIMIZATION _____ 198

    STRATEGY #2: IMAGE _____ 200

    STRATEGY #3: SUPPLIER DIVERSITY _____ 202

    STRATEGY #4: REGIONAL/COMMUNITY ENGAGEMENT _____ 204

    STRATEGY #5: STRATEGIC PARTNERSHIPS _____ 205

    STRATEGY #6: TRAINING & DEVELOPMENT ____ 209

    D&I SCORECARDS _____ 210

CHAPTER 14: NEW-SCHOOL LEADERSHIP FOR THE 21st
CENTURY _____ 219

    L = Lifelong Learner_____ 226

    E = Engagement _____ 228

    A = Ahead of the Curve _____ 229

    D = Diversity & Inclusion _____ 230

    E = Empathy_____ 231

    R = Relationship Management_____ 233

    S = Social Media Presence _____ 236

    H = High Energy _____ 237

    I = Influence & Enrollment _____ 238

    P = Platinum Rule _____ 240

    MUST-HAVE—VISION _____ 242

    MUST-HAVE—PURPOSE: Why_____ 243

    MUST-HAVE—PASSION _____ 244

    MUST-HAVE—GOOD COMMUNICATION SKILLS 245

    MUST-HAVE—MANAGEMENT SKILLS _____ 247

CHAPTER 15: STUDY STRATEGIES _____ 250

CHAPTER 16: THE CAE TEST DAY _____ 257

CHAPTER 17: SUMMARY & CONCLUSION	261
REFERENCES & RESOURCES	265
ABOUT THE AUTHOR	268
INDEX	286
ENDNOTES	282

CHAPTER 1

WHAT IS THE CAE?

For over fifty years, the Certified Association Executive credential has served to recognize the high professional standards, individual executive performance, and significant management knowledge of those professionals engaged in the management of American and international associations. It is accorded only by the American Society of Association Executives (ASAE: www.asaecenter.org)—the Center for Association Leadership.

You may already be a member of the ASAE, which represents more than 21,000 association executives who work in over 10,000 organizations. Or you may be considering the benefits of joining this prestigious professional organization. Its members manage leading trade associations, individual professional membership societies, and volunteer organizations across the United States, primarily organized under Section 501-c-6 of the Federal tax code, along with those leading philanthropic organizations that have been organized under section 501-c-3, although the ASAE has members all over the world.

The ASAE was founded in order to "advance, improve, promote and protect the profession of association management, and those professionals who manage business, trade, professional, philanthropic, scientific, educational, technical, social welfare, agricultural, and other nonprofit organizations; provide opportunities for the exchange of expertise, experiences and opinions through meetings, communications, education, research, and publications for nonprofit organization management professionals"; and "assist and encourage nonprofit organizations to reach the highest levels of effectiveness, efficiency, and achievement for their constituencies and society." As part of its efforts to "develop and encourage high standards of professional conduct among nonprofit organization management professionals," it instituted the qualifications and examination for the CAE™. To date, over 4,000 executives have achieved this credential. They represent some of the very most effective association leaders in the world, and the most qualified executives managing non-profit institutions in the U.S. and fifty additional countries.

There is a body called the CAE Commission that is comprised of ASAE members; it is responsible for overseeing the entire CAE certification program and credentialing process. This committee establishes and enforces the policies and standards for the certification which are then implemented by the staff at the ASAE. It is the CAE Commission that will issue to you your own credential, once you complete the qualification, application, and examination processes. When you receive confirmation that you have met all of the criteria established by the

Commission, you, too, will be considered a certified association executive!

CAE Benefits

The CAE credential is a significant undertaking, but one that offers a C-suite executive or aspirant considerable benefits. First, you have the opportunity to verify all that you know and can do through an organization that is fully independent of your own employer or professional field. When applying for a new position or promotion, you will be able to point beyond your immediate supervisor or references to this respected outside source as confirmation that you are capable, knowledgeable, and prepared to undertake new or expanded responsibilities.

Second, just preparing for the CAE alone offers you a unique opportunity for personal and professional development, and allows you to deepen your mastery of various aspects of association management that you may not yet have been taught or assigned. You are certain to garner new knowledge and understanding through the reading, review, and networking required to study for this exam. As a side benefit, you'll be able to implement new best practices and strategies in your current position, and enhance your decision-making abilities just through the process of applying to be a CAE candidate.

Third, this prestigious credential will qualify you for new professional situations or positions that may offer you increased responsibilities or enhanced compensation as you advance in your career. More and more, we need new and expanded professional credentials in order to make our resume or profile stand out to executive search firms and in professional social media. The CAE certificate is respected, quantifiable, and distinguished. So a fourth and additional benefit of the CAE credential is the pride that you'll be able to take in the achievement of a substantial goal, and the self-confidence that comes from recognizing a job well done.

Many times you will be supported in your undertaking of the CAE examination by your current employer. They, too, reap considerable benefits from having a Certified Association Executive on their staff. The ASAE has shown how executives with this credential can be counted on for greater productivity than many of their peers, for example. Your employer can use your certification as part of the competitive advantage that they offer their board of directors, members, funders, or others that evaluate the capacity of your organization to realize its mission.

If you are being considered for a position with a new association, being a Certified Association Executive may assure your future employer that you will need far less management and training time to integrate smoothly into your new environment. The CAE credential speaks for the wide base of skills and understanding that you bring with you to an institution or organization.

Prerequisites for the CAE

The ASAE and its CAE Commission identify the requirements for your becoming eligible to take the bi-annual test to become a CAE. These are modified and enhanced from time to time, so I recommend that you check in at the ASAE Center (www.asaecenter.org) as you begin your journey, just to confirm that you meet or are preparing to meet the most current prerequisites for becoming a Certified Association Executive.

You must meet all of the ASAE's requirements before you are eligible to register for the bi-annual examination. You must:

1. Be employed, or have been employed within the past five years, by a qualifying non-profit organization, or by an association management company. Qualifying non-profits include trade associations, professional societies, individual membership organizations, tribal or philanthropic organizations.
2. Hold a BA, or meet the CAE Commission's definition of "qualifying work experience" which is generally an additional eight years' work in the field; partial credit is given for undergraduate years of study completed.
3. Have at least three years of professional experience as the CEO of an organization, or

five years' as a staff member, plus have a Bachelor's degree.

4. Complete 100 hours of "broad-based qualifying experience" during the past five years, spread over the various domains that the CAE exam covers (the domains and their relative percentages are discussed in the chapters that follow).

5. Attest to uphold the ASAE's Standards of Conduct that are available at their website; with your signed confirmation, you also commit to disclose any felony convictions, and confirm that you have no felony convictions related to practicing association management.

So, in order to sit for the exam, you need to complete all of the above, then submit your application along with a non-refundable fee of $150. There are additional fees of $350 or $550 (depending on whether you are an ASAE member; totaling $500 or $700); these must be submitted concurrently with your application before the CAE Commission can review your materials and verify that you qualify to take the test. The second part of the fee is refunded if you don't meet all of the prerequisites or withdraw your application, and includes the entrance fee to take the exam one time.

Again, be certain to check all of the application details and deadlines at www.whatiscae.org, as fees and requirements may change.

CHAPTER 2

THE CAE EXAM—AN OVERVIEW

The CAE examination is designed to test your knowledge in the nine areas that encompass the skills and expertise expected of any Chief Staff Executive (CSE) at associations of various types or sizes. It is given twice each year on the first Fridays of May and December in a number of regional testing centers around the United States. The ASAE works with you if your organization has a number of executives (more than three) that qualify to take it at the same time, and makes provisions for candidates that need to travel long distances to the testing center or have other special requirements.

The test is four hours long, and has 200 multiple-choice questions about the day-to-day practice of American association professionals, based on a job analysis performed by the Association and CAE Commission. Unlike the SATs and GREs of your earlier academic career, your scoring for the CAE test is not relative to others that sit for the examination that day. There is a passing score established by the CAE Commission's panel of experts who determine the thresholds of basic competence in these nine aspects or areas of association management. Your test will be graded within six to eight weeks, and you will learn only whether you pass or fail, unless you don't meet the minimum passing score, in which case you'll be offered a report that explains where you succeeded and failed in each domain.

You may retake the test as many times as you choose, although there is a $250 retake fee each time that you do. If you do not pass the exam within a year of submitting your application materials, you will need to renew them and re-qualify as a CAE candidate. Information about hand grading and the appeals process is available in the CAE Program Candidate Handbook available free, online, at the Center website, www.asaecenter.org.

The ambition of this book, however, is to prepare you for the exam, and to give you study and test-taking strategies so that you are successful the very first time!

First, let's review the domains or content areas that the exam covers, and how much of your qualifying experience and percentage of test questions will be dedicated to each domain. After that, I will explain each domain in depth, along with ways to gain the knowledge or experience that you need to answer the questions in each area.

Preparing for the CAE Exam

The first step towards a successful experience with the CAE exam is to map out a course of study that culminates in your target test date, whether in summer or winter. Concurrent with your test preparation, you will need to complete and submit your CAE application that documents your eligibility, education, and work experience. Once your application is approved, you have the chance to sit for the exam during the next two test cycles, but since they are six months apart you may want to calendar the ideal date for your professional and personal life, and then work backwards to design your preparation schedule.

As with any study or review program, your success at retaining and incorporating the content of the CAE information and in being ready to recall and represent it on test day starts with your initial organization and commitment to the project. My recommendation is that you use the next sections of this book to gather first an overview of the exam content, and then schedule a weekly or monthly target of readings and review including the online CAE Candidate Handbook, designed around each of the nine domains.

In addition to mapping out a strategy for study, you may also want to organize a study group of like-minded Association Executives in your area. Discussing your readings and questions with a peer group can make your test preparation even more pleasurable; it can also provide new opportunities to network and help you set benchmarks over your study period that are supported and encouraged by regularly scheduled meetings with others on your path.

While your professional experience and knowledge is the basis of your CAE credential, there is a recommended list of outside reading that has been compiled by the CAE Commission. The ASAE reports that the most successful applicants who have taken their exam have used the recommended readings as the focal point for their study and professional development. The CAE Authoritative Literature list was last updated in October 2012, and was compiled by the Commission in order to prepare you both to be a Chief Staff Executive and to complete the CAE exam. (It can be found at http://goo.gl/GUz01g.) It is not the *only* source of questions on your examination, but the readings are selected to clarify the content areas and positions that the test will cover, and to give you direction for your preparation. Download the list today!

There are only 16 books on the current list, so I do recommend that you dive into those immediately. The current CAE Core Resources is a sample list of five books that the organization considers closely aligned with the content you will find on the exam. It includes:

1. *Association Law Handbook,* 5th edition
2. *Professional Practices in Association Management,* 2nd edition with 3rd edition due out in early 2015
3. *The Jossey-Bass Handbook of Nonprofit Leadership and Management,* 3rd edition
4. *How to Read Nonprofit Financial Statements,* 2nd edition, new edition expected in early 2016
5. *Membership Essentials: Recruitment, Retention, Roles,* new edition expected in December 2015

I also suggest that you make a regular practice of reading *Associations NOW* magazine, published by the ASAE & The Center, as a way to share in current trends and best practices that will also be helpful in your test preparation.

If you have an opportunity to attend the ASAE's Great Ideas Conference (described at the Center website), generally scheduled for a weekend in early March of each year, you will add another chance to network and expand your understanding of state-of-the-art thinking about association management strategies during your exam preparation process. It is designed to be a relaxed but professional event that takes you out of your daily responsibilities so that you can be exposed to new ideas, people, creativity, and practices that may be great to integrate into your current job, not just apply to the CAE examination. Oftentimes a supportive employer will encourage and supplement your attendance at this annual event.

There are state and regional SAE meetings that can also be valuable in your test prep process. Also consider attending any non-profit law workshops that are offered in your area, whether sponsored by your local SAE organization or by other non-profit service centers like the Center for Non-profit Management in Southern California (http://cnmsocal.org/), the Kellogg School's Center for Non-profit Management center in Chicago (http://www.kellogg.northwestern.edu/research/nonprofit.aspx), the Support Center in New York's Tri-State area (http://supportcenteronline.org/), or similar resources in your own area.

I recommend that you include your exam study periods, study group meetings, and all dates and deadlines in your professional and personal calendar from the beginning. This formalizes your process, carves out the time that you need to read and review key material on a schedule that progresses to your test date, and organizes your thinking.

It will also help to minimize anxiety: you know what you need to do when you need to do it, and you can rest assured that you have thought through a comfortable schedule where everything can get done in advance of your exam. Build in some wiggle room for yourself, too, of course: there are always unanticipated things that come up, in work and life, that blow up your schedule for a little while, right?

CHAPTER 3

CAE TEST DOMAINS

There are nine major content areas that the CAE test will cover, in varying proportions. They are called Domains by the ASAE, and they are periodically reviewed and adjusted. A detailed outline of the nine domains that will be used to guide the composition of the CAE exam through December 2014 is available in the Candidate Handbook on the ASAE Center website. Check for annual updates and adjustments.

In the following chapters, I will cover the essential details and study areas for each of the nine domains. Each content area has its own important key terms and recommended outside reading. They are, including an approximate percentage (in parentheses) of the test that will be devoted to each area:

Domain 1: ORGANIZATIONAL MANAGEMENT (14-16%)

Domain 2: LEADERSHIP (14-16%)

Domain 3: ADMINISTRATION (14-16%)

Domain 4: KNOWLEDGE MANAGEMENT & RESEARCH (4-6%)

Domain 5: GOVERNANCE AND STRUCTURE (9-11%)

Domain 6: PUBLIC POLICY, GOVERNMENT RELATIONS, AND COALITION BUILDING (6-8%)

Domain 7: MEMBERSHIP DEVELOPMENT (10-12%)

Domain 8: PROGRAMS, PRODUCTS, AND SERVICES (12-14%)

Domain 9: MARKETING, PUBLIC RELATIONS, AND COMMUNICATIONS (8-10%)

You should plan to dedicate at least one full week, initially, to reading this material and the reading list chapters or books associated with each domain topic. That would comprise your first nine weeks of study and review for the CAE exam. Then you can begin taking sample tests to identify the areas where you are strong and well-versed, and others where you want to devote additional study, review, reading; it is a good idea to supplement your knowledge by meeting with local professionals who have expertise in the best practices for those subject areas, as well.

The following chapters will give you an overview of the domains and their subsections, along with key terminology and mnemonics that you should understand or memorize.

CHAPTER 4

DOMAIN 1: ORGANIZATIONAL MANAGEMENT

The first CAE content domain umbrellas a great deal of strategic management thinking and core concepts related to marketing and branding, as well as financial management and future visioning through strategic planning. (Marketing is also discussed in more depth in the chapter on Domain 8, while branding is further explained in the exploration of Domain 9). As with so much of what our board of directors and funders require these days, a facility with metrics and measurements is key to a lot of the learning for this content area.

First, as in any corporate analysis whether for-profit or non-profit, you must understand how to recognize and articulate the core competencies of your association or organization. Senior managers and their boards of directors are responsible for ensuring that your institutional activities and operations put these competencies to their best use, and that they are supported both internally and externally.

When you have a solid understanding of your own institution's strengths, you may also be able to identify your weaknesses or strategic needs. Particularly in a 21st century approach to non-profit success, you want to be able to evaluate and align or partner with other entities (e.g., non-profit corporations, foundations, local or regional groups) that can enhance your work or support your mission. **Collaborations** are relationships where "multiple parties work together on a project, and where their foundation is workability."

The way that you manage—from incorporating best practices to applying effective management theories within your unique institution—are key concepts in this domain, including **logical project management processes** (from analyzing needs to planning and prioritization, then program development and implementation, management and evaluation).

Be familiar with the most current and varied **fundamental theories** of management, organizational behavior and employee motivation. These include, but aren't limited to: "Maslow's Hierarchy of Needs; Douglas McGregor's Theory X and Theory Y; Ken Blanchard and Paul Hersey's Situational Leadership Theory; and Edward De Bono's Six Thinking Hats." Tools, both quantitative and qualitative, are essential that measure how your programs and processes are achieving the goals set by you and your board, including quality control procedures and processes for innovation and change.

Recognize that a Chief Staff Executive also needs a process to address **organizational uncertainties** which includes a broad, macro assessment of "key questions about the future"; then "isolates real uncertainty from perceived uncertainty"; identifies any biases to addressing your uncertainties; then "develops leadership and the right culture," and "changes organizational systems that block success."

You should know the mechanisms by which **organizational success can be blocked.** These include rigid organizational structures that fail to incorporate future-looking demographics and flexible decision making; "results-based compensation structures that focus executives in the past rather than on potential opportunities"; and "static present/net value analysis," which is a "rigid financial tool." Flexibility is generally the better institutional policy.

Board relations and management are a content area unto themselves, but as regards general management, you need to understand how to work with your board to develop a **succession plan** for top staff leaders. These plans include "what qualities are needed and who will succeed the current leader;

they are ready to implement "when a term ends, a retirement is announced, or someone resigns."

You will also need to master the elements of leadership recruitment and the components of annual assessments or evaluations. For this and other general management concepts, it is important to understand how and where to develop a strong network of association-executive peers, including the ways in which you can utilize this resource for better management.

While we often think of our organizations and their missions in terms of social change, strategies for change and innovation are essential tools for Association Executives *within* their associations, as well. Be certain to understand the ways in which change comes about, both inside and out: top down, bottom up, through a segment or representative sample of a constituency or staff, and throughout an entire enterprise by way of a complete overhaul. Review the book *7 Measures of Success: What Remarkable Associations Do That Others Don't* on the "Authoritative Literature" recommended reading list.

Your analysis of an organization's core competencies and unique value proposition is intimately linked to the scope of your membership and/or customer market. How to identify target segments and key or potential stakeholders is an essential component of mastering the marketing & branding aspects of association management, as are the concepts of preferred positioning, and how to develop a distinctive, rather than a fuzzy or redundant, brand. **Branding** is a "marketing process that incorporates singular look, feel, and message in building a belief about your association and its products." It communicates the uniqueness of your organization or program, so it inspires purchasing behavior because there is no product like yours.

You need to understand how to conduct an environmental scan, how to research and identify tactics for increasing both your members' and your funders' return on their investment (ROI), and you need to be able to develop and implement a marketing plan. (For a complete list of a great marketing plan's components, along with strategies for its development, please consult the John Burnett book, *Nonprofit Marketing Best Practices,* on the CAE Authoritative Literature List.)

Financial management is a very familiar component of every senior association executive's duties. You can expect to be tested on the ways that you arrange and supervise your accounting services, and how to develop, pass or recommend, implement, and manage your annual and project budgets. You need to understand **financial projections,** which are generally speculative forecasts of future financial results that "should be based on credible assumptions, a conservative projection of revenue, and an aggressive projection of expense."

All financial performance in an organization needs to have systems for oversight and monitoring, including the most efficacious tools and metrics for evaluation, reporting, and independent evaluation. These include sub-components like how to calculate revenues per project or per member, or the percentage of retention that can be linked to a specific campaign. **Financial key indicators** are sometimes selected by leaders to provide quantitative measurements that "indicate a fairly accurate picture of the organization in relation to its strategic plan." Examples include the "number of new members, accounts, new business starts, and organizational members participating in the program, plus percent of retained members."

You'll need to know the components of a clear, accurate, and complete reporting system that accommodates the needs of your board, your staff, sometimes your members, and, in most cases, your funders., and the differences between a cash and accrual system. You may do your accounting on an **accrual basis,** which "recognizes revenues when earned and expenses when incurred," or **cash-basis,** which "recognizes revenues when cash is received and expenses when cash is expended." Best Practice is to use accrual accounting, because it gives you a better cash flow projection.

A **Combined Cash & Accrual Statement** records some transactions, like unpaid bills, on an accrual basis, while it records others, like uncollected income, on a cash basis. These can be done between monthly statements, then converted to accrual at the end of the month for accounting purposes. Your **association reserves** are "net assets minus liabilities"; your surplus that is often protected by your Board, and may be incorporated into your annual budget.

Review all of the elements of a **chart of accounts**, the system for organizing financial data that lists "all of the line item accounts being used by your organization," and assigns each one a number so that you can ensure "sound financial management and reporting" by making "accurate and appropriate entries into correct accounts." Ensuring that these procedures are followed is key to your financial management best practice.

Understand the purpose of all the various accounting statements including balance sheets, financial positioning statements, income and expense reports, and cash flow statements: how they are created, what they communicate, and how to manage through this information.

Bone up on key financial management ratios including your **Liquidity ratio,** which "measures the organization's ability to pay its short-term obligations; **current ratio,** which "measures the current assets divided by current liabilities;" **Profitability ratio,** which "measures the profits and loss over a specific period of time"; the **coverage ratio,** which "measures the projections for the interest and principal payments to long-term creditors and investors"; and the **Activity ratio** or **efficiency ratio,** which "measures the resources required to carry out certain activities.

Your **annual audit** engages an auditor to verify the amounts that are included in the financial reports that are maintained by an association's management. Your records have to agree with the report certified by your auditor. Be certain that you understand the different types of audits available to non-profit organizations, and which are required by different sorts of funders or contracts. A **clean audit** is "an opinion providing the highest level of assurance that the *Statement of Financial Position* fairly represents the organization's financial position, the *Statement of Activities* fairly presents the results of the organization's operations; and the *Statement of Cash Flows* fairly presents its cash flows."

Your **statement of financial position** will summarize your association's financial makeup, its assets, liabilities, and net assets, at a specific moment in time. It has also been called a **balance sheet,** and includes three classes of funds: **unrestricted funds,** which is income that may be used in any way management decides (**capital gains** are reported as unrestricted, unless there are "explicit donor restrictions" or some applicable state law); **temporarily restricted net assets,** which are contributed to your organization with limits imposed by your donors, either that they be used for a specific purpose, or within a specified time frame; and **permanently restricted net assets** with a specific non-expiring purpose, that never shift to the organization, like an endowment.

Your **statement of activities,** also called a **profit/loss statement** or **statement of revenue and expenses,** shows your association's month by month financial activity, including amounts of generated revenue, incurred expenses, and any net loss or net income. The **statement of cash flows** documents cash disbursements and receipts that come about in an organization due to its investments, operations, and any financing activities during a specific period of time. **Cash** is so important in an organization's financial health that this statement helps managers to analyze your financial flexibility, while creditors can evaluate whether your association is able to "generate positive future cash flow to meet its obligations and its need for external financing."

The other type of audit is an **unqualified audit.** This is also "an opinion providing the highest level of assurance that an audit can provide," but with "attention to a particular matter." It discloses additional financial statements, or it "draws attention to an additional important matter." A **management letter** is issued by your independent auditor, and will communicate to you and your board any "areas that management needs to address in order to come into compliance with GAAP accounting practices."

Review the three stages to an audit, the three types of auditor's reports, and understand the Generally Accepted Accounting Practices (GAAP) as they apply to association management. Confirm for yourself an association's tax obligations, non-profit status notwithstanding.

Review how to calculate **UBIT** (Unrelated Business Income Tax), which is "income derived from a regularly conducted trade or business activity that is not significantly related to the tax-exempt purpose of the organization. (Remember: if more than 30% of your budget falls under this category, you will jeopardize your tax-exempt status; your organization must file a 990-T in addition to your 990 when you have more than $1,000 in annual gross from UBI).

Know what your policies should be regarding a member's tax-deductibility of your services or meetings, and how to review a standard 990 Federal tax filing. Even as a not-for-profit, your association may have **taxable functions** like "dues related to lobbying; expense deductibility from attendance at association meetings; income derived from real estate; income produced form non-dues sources of revenue, and advertising."

Non-profits are required to maintain **open information,** which includes making your 990 or **990EZ** (the simplified form for associations with gross revenues under $100,000 and total assets under $25,000) available for public inspection, so that donors can verify allocations of donations to administrative expense. (Members are entitled to your minutes, if requested, but member lists are the association's property and may be withheld from non-members.) Your tax forms are due on the 15th day of the fifth month after the association's fiscal year ends.

The "best practice in **Strategic Program Budgeting** involves salary and overhead allocation so that the CSE knows the "true profitability of your association's products and services." To achieve this, you need to know how to do a systematic study that relates "allocation of staff time to program categories", prorating your overhead to the program.

Your **operating budget** is the basic "day-to-day financial plan" that projects revenue and expenses for the organization and its programs. **Overhead** is any "expense incurred that is not an actual, direct expense for a specific program," like your phones and computers, rent and maintenance, services like accounting and insurance. You may also have a **capital budget,** one that plans for "long-term expenditures like land, buildings or equipment;" this budget includes depreciation and **capital expenditures** on major additions or improvements to your facilities.

On the Authoritative Literature list, the Lang and Berson book, *How to Read Nonprofit Financial Statements,* dives into these financial management matters in detail, while others of the books have important sections on general and financial topics to be reviewed like *The Jossey-Bass Handbook for Nonprofit Leadership and Management,* chapters 19-21.

You need to have a basic understanding of investment policies and activities, and the capacity to evaluate and engage the services of an investment management firm. Developing a policy for an institutional reserve is part of financial management, as are the skills for examining and extrapolating from external economic factors as well as internal budget realities when doing financial planning, or developing investment or reserve policies.

You must be able to identify the salient components of a financial or accounting handbook, including the strongest internal financial controls possible for an institution of your size. Know how to ensure **segregation of duties,** which specifies the accounting practice that "no individual controls all four aspects of any financial transaction": check requests or initiation; approvals to pay or authorizations; keeping the checkbook or asset custody; and posting or recording of transactions.

Your handbook will include an anti-fraud policy and the tenets of **Sarbanes-Oxley;** the two provisions that directly impact your association and its financial policies are the "whistle-blower protection provision, which prohibits interference with a person who reports a potential infraction to a federal law enforcement agency," and "the prohibition of document destruction upon the commencement of federal investigation." But additional conflict of interest and fraud protection policies, in light of Sarbanes-Oxley, may be relevant to your association, including a specified code of ethics for financial officers, and certifications by the CEO and CFO about an organization's financial condition and internal controls.

Your handbook will align financial authority within your organization with appropriate executive responsibility, as well as provide for proper training in your organization's practices to those involved with financial management. The four financial

factors essential to solid internal controls are: "clear lines of authority"; "clear definition and acceptance of responsibility"; "authority commensurate with responsibility"; and "proper training." You should be able to demonstrate that you know how to monitor and maintain the level of cash flow necessary for the day-to-day and month-to-month needs of your organization's operations.

In this subject area, you will also be expected to know how to evaluate or manage subsidiaries and other corporate entities like a 501-c-6 membership organization that can lobby; a 501-c-3 non-profit foundation, if yours isn't one already, for scientific or educational purposes with little or limited lobbying ability; and perhaps a for-profit affiliate that provides business services in exchange for a new revenue source to your parent association.

A tax-exempt organization can own "100% of a **for-profit subsidiary,** provided the two entities engage in separate activities, have separate boards of directors, separate books and records, and separate bank accounts, and the subsidiary is not an 'alter ego' of the parent organizations. "You should know the five key **reasons to form** such a **subsidiary**:

   a. To engage in activities that are not permitted under your bylaws or charter
   b. To offer new services to a niche or market segment
   c. To bring additional revenue sources to your organization
   d. To increase your non-profit's scope or capacity
   e. To protect or shelter your organization from a potential financial setback, downturn or failure

In their 2012 adjustment of the CAE exam content, the Commission included in this domain an understanding of both globalization and strategic planning. In the first regard, social, cultural, and economic trends—both macro and micro—often have an impact on an association and its constituents. In order to provide proper management and strategic planning, you will be expected to have the skills to analyze, interpret, and communicate these challenges in terms of how they may impact your organization and its prospects.

While your current association may not have global reach or impact, you will be expected to understand the ways in which an executive utilizes trends, research, and current legal realities to participate or expand into a global initiative. You should be able to assess the ways in which global issues, both inside your organization and out, may impact your stakeholders and members, products, programs or services.

As regards Strategic Planning, first you need to know that organizations plan in order to assess their strengths and weaknesses, to identify present and future member needs, and to develop or implement great products or services to meet those needs. **Visioning** is the imagining of a desired future, and a "commitment to rethink and review the organization holistically, while scanning and planning for the long-term results in an organization." It must begin with a commitment by the leadership.

A Strategic Plan may have **growth objectives,** sometimes called "doing the right things," which are the "abilities to identify critical issues and opportunities that can change and develop an organization for the better, strategies that energize and maximize a strategic plan. Or planning may have **maintenance objectives,** or "doing things right," which is "important for maintaining and sustaining growth."

There are set of characteristics to most Plans, and six standard steps in the Strategic Planning process. A CSE must first define the process, inform the staff, and confirm the Board's approval and participation. Research on market and service trends as they relate to an institution and its stakeholders may be conducted by staff, or by outside advisors that are selected and contracted to participate in or lead your Strategic Planning preparation, retreat, or report writing. The mission of your organization may need to be reconfirmed or modified, and even in its original form, it often inspires the goals that you and your board identify for your next two to five years.

The process of strategic planning often articulates or reconfirms an association's **values,** or the beliefs at the heart of the organization; and its **vision,** that image to which the association aspires. The SP process should develop an action plan and priorities, then allocate the time and financial resources of the organization to realize its objectives. It may be necessary to develop new funding strategies during this process in order to address the needs and ambitions identified in the Plan; be prepared to identify them. Evaluation and revision steps are often built in to your Plan, as well, so that your association can either make adjustments during the Plan period, or recognize the need to start again. A useful mnemonic is SPIE: Scan, Plan, Implement, Evaluate.

You must be familiar with the traditional org analysis tools like the **Environmental Scan,** which is inseparable from Strategic Planning. It is a "systematic effort to obtain information about the world that will affect an organization," as is considered important to "managing change and avoiding costly mistakes." It looks at the "macro environment," which is the "larger space shared with other organizations and professions"; the "association industry environment and organizational trends, like evolving governance, structures, operational practices, services to members, technology trends, and competition"; the "environment in which the members operate," which is the profession itself; and the "association's immediate operating environment," including "internal trends and issues that need to be addressed like governance and structure, leadership, management and administration, internal and external relations, communications, programs, and services."

The six-step model of doing **environmental scanning** involves: "Plan, review the literature, brainstorm issues, do member surveys, and outreach to others; Scan the trends within your industry as well as the operating environment; Apply insights and interpret the trends to your association's strategy; Establish a framework for decision-making;

Identify the strategic issues that the association should address; and Develop strategies."

Organizations often discover or discuss their **response models** in this process: **fluidity** "encourages a paradigm where the marketplace decides an association's actions and priorities"; **flexibility** "involves ways to move assets easily in order to quickly reshape direction"; and **nimbleness** makes "decision-making processes operate more quickly and more maneuverable." Best management practices encourage CSEs to seek out and upgrade structures like membership, governance, event, financial and informational structures that inhibit nimbleness.

Additional tools to review are the SWOT analysis, and applicable Market Analysis strategies that are also discussed in later domains. Know what sorts of performance metrics that can be used, on an ongoing basis, to evaluate a Strategic Plan's effectiveness. You should also be able to articulate a number of the challenges that associations encounter when they do not undertake regular planning of this sort.

I recommend that you review chapter 12 in *Professional Practices in Association Management* on tactical planning, and chapter 17 on research and statistics. The *Association Law Book* dedicates chapters to statistical surveys, joint research, and "The Cooperative Research and Production Act" that are also relevant to planning practices review. Additional chapters in the Cox *Professional Practices* that are important for this domain include chapter 2-3, 5, 13 and 29. The Jacobs *Law Handbook* includes chapters 1, 6, 8-10 on policy and procedures, Sarbanes-Oxley, and statements of purpose, along with fiduciary responsibilities. The *7 Measures of Success,* as I mentioned, should also be read in the context of this subject area, while the *The Jossey-Bass Handbook* dedicates chapter 8 to Strategic Planning.

CHAPTER 5

DOMAIN 2: LEADERSHIP

This domain covers the components of excellent leadership, including ethics, negotiation, and sophisticated interpersonal relations. It will comprise 14-16% of the CAE exam. The questions that pertain to this subject area may appear to cover membership or governance, but in fact are testing your understanding of the best practices for decision making, organizational culture, collaborative leadership, and managing people.

SPIE applies here, as well: a good leader Scans, Plans, Implements, and Evaluates at any opportunity. A good leader is aware that, while communications involve M2M (member to member) and S2S (staff to staff), a CSE communicates with other Chief Executives. And a good leader knows that, in order to **build trust,** they must achieve results, act with integrity, and demonstrate concern.

Understand the key processes of management and leadership. The former is decision-making, creative thinking, directing and controlling, listening, problem solving, implementing and technology. The latter is inspiring creativity, ensuring understanding, supporting, empowering, humanizing, and resolving conflicts. Organizations that "avoid conflict and confrontation cannot function as an aligned team."

By contrast, teams that engage in **Constructive Confrontation** have "lively, interesting meetings, extract and use team members' ideas; solve real problems quickly, minimize politics, and put critical topics on the table for discussion." Know the ways in which constructive confrontation can bring teams together through creating an honest environment where you can manage conflict.

Seven possible **leadership competencies** include servant leadership, creating and communicating vision, promoting and initiating change, building partnerships, valuing diversity, managing information and technology, and achieving balance.

A number of the recommended reading books look at effective leadership strategies and **organizational culture**, which is the "set of policies, practices, values and expectations that define and guide a workplace or organization." The supplementary essays and reviews of innovative models should be surveyed, as well. These include ways to gather and examine both qualitative and quantitative data in the course of decision making.

Leadership through data recognizes that making decisions in knowledge-based non-profit associations will only be as valuable "as the quality of the information on which those decisions are based." You need to build databases to guide your management decisions about everything from strategy and policy to programs and delivery systems.

Leadership through data involves a "continuous and integrated consideration of member needs, wants and preferences; capacity and strategic position of organizations; external marketplace dynamics and realities; and fairness and appropriateness of choices."

The CSE is often called a "servant-leader," given your responsibility to serve at the pleasure of a Board. You are still the organization's leader, however, and must always command the larger picture of that complex, inter-related system that is your institution and the full field with which it interacts. As an association leader, you are responsible for holding this "big picture" vision, and for understanding the benefits of implementing a collaborative leadership model as a way to invite many perspectives, keep an open mind, support your intention to influence not control, and be accountable to stakeholders and mission.

Participant Management is a widely esteemed leadership practice. It seeks to involve anyone affected by the outcomes of a decision-making process, to at least some degree. As a leader, you may accept or modify any stakeholder's evaluation of a problem or practice, but it is essential that you give these voices considered evaluation in your analysis.

Know the elements of **Active Listening,** which "requires being in the present moment, engaged with the speaker rather than thinking about your response; noticing when the body language does not match the words spoken, or the passion expressed is not aligned with the issue discussed, then enquire about the incongruence." Sometimes active listening involves paraphrasing what you have heard, in order to acknowledge the speaker and ensure understanding.

You may need to model and encourage effective participation for the members of your staff and board. Modeling a balanced lifestyle with appropriate, healthy boundaries is equally important for you to do, as an effective leader. You also need to know how to **maximize volunteer capacity,** that is, how to "assess how you use volunteers in and train them for decision-making processes," so that they can have the "minimum time involvement, maximum influence, and major benefit" that they seek. Since volunteers offer their time and energy generally because they want to make a difference, you need to know how to help them do that, whether it is through providing "skill and conceptual development in governance and leadership, team building, or cultural orientation in order to maximize the potential."

Proactive leadership is also essential in a CSE: identifying and anticipating risk, keeping your eyes on the long-range view of an organization's decisions and programs, and projecting a preferred future. Strong leaders keep their Boards and staff looking forward, they engage their volunteer leadership in discussions about positive and negative trends in the foreseeable future, and they aim to do things because they are important, not because they are necessary.

Informed intuition is a forward-thinking strategy that involves "sensitivity to member needs, expectations, and preferences; foresight into the likely evolution of the member's environments; insight into the capacity and strategic position of the organization; and consideration of the ethical dimensions of choices." The Robert Herman handbook, and the Hesselbein, Goldsmith and Somerville essay anthology offer insights into the leadership strategies that you should understand, in preparing for questions from this domain.

You are charged with establishing the ethical framework and expectations for all of your association's staff and volunteer behavior, including maximum transparency, and to design an effective method for communicating these standards both inside of your organization and out. Know the components of a Conflict of Interest Policy, whether included in your By Laws/Amendments, or as a stand-alone document. Apply the ASAE's own Standards of Conduct in order to model ethical behavior. Know how to utilize the Ethics Four-Way Test:

1. Is it LEGAL?
2. Is it BALANCED?
3. How does it make me FEEL about myself?

4. How will it LOOK on the front page of *The Huffington Post*?

Ethical dilemmas will arise. Know the resources and wisdom that you can tap, as their CSE, in order to parse each question and respond with the highest degree of integrity. On your reading list, the Jennifer Baker and Janice Dahl book *How Are Your Ethics?* offers some essential information on this topic, as does chapter 9 of *The Jossey-Bass Handbook*.

An understanding of the priorities and benefits of diversity are critical to association and general business management. Diversity should be a core personal and institutional value of any organization and its CSE. The 21st century workforce is heterogeneous and, in many regards, majority minority. Good leadership ensures that decision making is made with consideration of a diverse and representative set of perspectives. Your Board should include or solicit diverse points of view, and may need to be reminded by a CSE that their decisions should reflect the diversity of your membership or constituency. Even unanimous votes for action should involve consensus building, and the engagement of diverse, contrary, or oppositional points of view.

You must know how to incorporate diversity in all of an association's services and programs, communications, marketing, and outreach strategies. **Diversity** includes sensitivities across the broad spectrum of minority and protected classes including ethnicity and race, age, gender and sexual orientation, appearance and disability, geography and nationality, and even professional levels. Optimally, "it is about inclusiveness of differences at all levels of the organization." I go into more detail on approaching diversity and inclusion in a future chapter.

You will be responsible for knowing how to create an inclusive culture within an organization, one that engenders respect and understanding of diverse voices and visions. Develop your personal leadership strategies for inspiring productivity and collaboration between people with very different backgrounds and perspectives.

As a staff leader, you will need to demonstrate how to manage cross-functional work teams, and the differences in work styles between departments, silos, and teams. You are responsible for the possible ways to advance your staff's and volunteers' professional and personal development. These include coaching, career counseling, mentoring, and leadership development.

Mentoring is a best practice in "developing leadership capacity" for "emerging leaders and new board members." It involves assigning teachers, on a one-on-one basis, to model behaviors of leadership and how to follow through on commitments. You need to know the elements of effective group facilitation, including the differences between consensus, compromise, and collaboration. Board activities and processes often need the CSE to serve as staff facilitator, as well, in partnership with the chair and committee heads. In addition, please review the various systems for conflict management.

Negotiation is the process for getting and keeping agreements. It is considered successful if each party has something to gain, and can also surrender things that they admit are not essential. Win/win means that everyone wins <u>equitably,</u> not necessarily <u>equally.</u> **Collaborative win/win negotiations to solve problems and challenges** follow a "principled approach to negotiations," and ensure that there is mutual gain to all parties involved.

Successful negotiators remember that any terms can be changed, there is a scarce resource (people, money, time, space) at the center of the discussions, and all of the parties involved in a negotiation need to have something to gain. The three principles of Negotiation are:

1. The first speaker sets the tone
2. The person who asks the most questions determines the direction and content
3. Good negotiators must state and understand the case of all parties

Research Karrass' Golden Rules of Negotiation: there are eleven of them, and they are very useful. You should also be familiar with elements of negotiating your own employment contract. There are two sections dedicated to that in the *Association Law Book.*

The Jossey-Bass Handbook dedicates chapters 6 and 7 to leadership, and the Hesselbein, Goldsmith and Somerville anthology, *Leading for Innovation,* should be reviewed for this domain.

In addition, Chapter 14 goes into my strategies for effective new-school leadership, as does my own book, *New-School Leadership: Making a Difference in the 21st Century,* available in paperback, eBook or audio. (Available on Amazon through this link: http://goo.gl/AJmdvV)

CHAPTER 6

DOMAIN 3: ADMINISTRATION

As your association's CSE, you have broad responsibility for the people and facilities, including your technology infrastructure. This domain's subject areas look closely at your capacity to manage your human resources, vendors, and the office, buildings, and technology plan. It will comprise 14-16% of the CAE exam.

While your leadership relationship to staff is often aspirational, encouraging them to attain their highest capabilities in service of your programs and mission, your **Human Resources** responsibilities are rooted in HR policies and procedures. You need to understand the components of a work environment that promotes strong staff communication and teamwork, as well as organizational effectiveness and efficiency so that your association accomplishes its goals and retains great personnel. The CSE needs to be clear about the chain of command within their organization, and delineate each internal job function, along with the position's organizational responsibilities.

You must ensure that your association's personnel policies, which elucidate the standards of conduct and decision making processes, are always connected to related procedures. All policies must be approved by the CSE and Board of Directors. Procedures are the "how to" of administering various policies, and are executed by your staff. One of your chief responsibilities is to communicate your institution's policies to your staff, and have them follow the prescribed procedures.

SPIE is a valuable strategy for the creation of policies and procedures: Scanning your organization, program or issue; Planning the appropriate policies;

Implementing the procedures with your staff; and then Evaluating the outcomes, consequences, or changing landscape. Another strategy or set of questions can be remembered as **LERP:** is it Legal, Ethical, Reasonable/Relational, and Practical/Procedural?

You need to understand the process for recruiting, hiring, and training new staff. Human resources are your most valuable asset, and need to be accorded the appropriate attention of a CSE. Develop a standardized approach to your staff recruitment in order to evaluate your candidates with consistency. **Factors in staff recruitment** include the salary for each position, and whether it is competitive for the work that is required; and the design of each job, including variety and opportunities for personal development or advancement. It also involves measuring each applicant's interest or emotional engagement with the organization's mission or social change issues, as well as their connection to or skills in the specialized area of a given position.

The HR factors that impact your ultimate success in staff recruitment, elements that candidates weigh as much as CSEs, include: salary and benefits including opportunities for professional development; reward or recognitions programs; fair treatment with care and concern from management; trust; and accountability that is instilled at every level of employee, supervisor or manager.

Recruitment can come about a number of ways: through job postings, referrals, or the internal process of job bidding, wherein someone informs HR that they are interested in a position that is already filled. You must be aware of the legal limitations on what questions are permissible in an interview; the PPAM (*Professional Practices in Association Management*) has pages that specify these criteria. You should know how to complete background checks, and the liability issues related to hiring. (If you do not hire someone based on information that they neglected to provide, you must inform them about what you discovered.)

A **contract** is a voluntary agreement between two or more individuals, and if it encompasses the five essential components, a legally binding relationship is forged. A contract includes an **offer, specific acceptance (mutual consent)**, and money or some other exchange of value in **consideration**. Contracts also need to be **mutual,** and the contracting parties need to have the authority (and be **competent**) to enter into such a binding agreement. In order to be **enforceable**, a contract also needs to be in writing.

Know the elements that should be included in all basic **Personnel files:** the employment application and resume, job descriptions, records relating to hiring and promotion, any training, letters of recognition, disciplinary notices, performance evaluations, exit interviews, and termination records. You should **not** include I-9 forms, insurance or medical records, child support garnishment information, litigation documents, worker's comp claims, requests for payroll verification, or reference checks.

Once staff is hired, you need to know the elements of a successful orientation program, and how to establish ongoing training that maintains and advances your staff's skills. The key elements of a **performance review process** are that it is formal, that it is written, and that it is regular. Ideally, when designed and implemented correctly, it maximizes your staff's performance. Wherever possible, it should include praise and be linked with increases in compensation. The CSE should know how to design a strategic compensation program that inspires and retains staff.

Where there are infractions or when a disciplinary process is necessary, everything up to and including termination must be in writing. As CSE, you are responsible for structuring a discipline and termination policy, then putting in place the correlating procedures that both ensure the fair and equitable treatment of your staff, and that mitigate the organization's exposure to risk.

An essential CSE responsibility that makes HR less stressful and performance reviews more valuable for the growth and well-being of the association, is to establish **consistency**: in timing, in standards, in approach. Apart from the annual review, **performance management** should include goal setting, day-to-day coaching, and regular appraisals of performance.

CSE termination and job security protections can be negotiated in a CSE employment contract, along with defining who is involved in CSE appraisals, what body/positions have the authority to terminate employment, notice, and severance issues. Know that the major factors that contribute to CSE termination are when the CSE "functions knowledgeably but behaves ineffectively," and when the CSE "focuses more on his or her own role than with doing a good job for the members."

A CSE must provide a safe work environment, and this includes your taking steps to prevent sexual harassment. **Sexual harassment** is any "unwelcome sexual advances, requests for sexual favors, or other verbal or physical conduct of a sexual nature." These requests or advances are considered sexual harassment if ever a condition of employment; if they involve an employment risk or consequence; or if an offensive job interference. Know how to provide a sexual harassment policy for your employees, board members and members, and design mechanisms for the reporting of complaints without fear of reprisal. Be prepared to investigate any complaints promptly and carefully, and in many cases implement sexual harassment sensitivity training in your workplace.

If you have the need for **staff reductions**, separate and apart from a disciplinary action or termination of an individual, there is a **legal checklist** to follow. Begin with a review of your personnel handbook, then map out any relevant issues. Be consistent and know all of the relevant laws regarding early retirement.

The *Worker Adjustment and Retraining Notification Act* (WARN) has a checklist in order to release employee claims in exchange for enhanced severance packages. It applies only if groups of employees have forty-five days to consider their offer, and seven days to revoke any acceptance. Consider any state regulations that impact dismissals, and prepare any notifications that fall under the *Consolidated Omnibus Budget Reconciliation Act* (COBRA) or pension notices, if you have employees affected in either regard. If you can offer opportunities to transfer to another branch or affiliate, consider that, along with any obligations that bind you under collective bargaining agreements.

Where a **termination** is considered necessary, know as CSE that this is a very sensitive issue and full of potential liabilities. Make yourself aware of whistle-blower protections, eligible disabilities, and anti-discrimination laws. Review the HR law sections of your CAE Exam prep books, and recognize that consulting an HR attorney in the event of a planned termination is both appropriate and wise.

You need to understand the function and responsibilities of the I-9 Employment Eligibility Verification form, including that it must be retained for three years after date of hire, or one year after employment ends; and both state and federal recordkeeping requirements. This includes FLSA, OSHA, etc. on the federal level; and state payroll taxes, etc. on the state. You must know all the relevant employment laws, and ensure compliance throughout your association in order to protect yourselves from the risk of fines or suits.

You also need to understand the various job descriptions as related to HR: full-time, part-time, temporary, contractors, exempt and non-exempt. **Non-exempt employees** must be paid minimum wage, at least, must keep time cards and take mandated break and lunch periods, and receive overtime for any hours that they work beyond forty (including daily lunch break) each week.

You must understand the terms under which the Department of Labor defines a **non-exempt** employee: there are numerous criteria, and they are very specific. **Exempt employees** that meet the DOL's definition of management are paid on a "salary" basis, that is, the same amount for each week of work regardless of the hours required.

Some employers are opting to use **compressed time**, wherein their employees may work four ten-hour days, or nine days over two weeks with one day off. Another HR option is **flextime**, where employees are allowed to vary their schedules so long as it works for the needs of the association. An additional employment option to understand is **co-employment,** created by Professional Employer Organizations (PEOs). Under this arrangement, staff are employees of both the association and the PEO, which is advantageous because: it offers staff better benefits, since the PEO is "able to give a small staff access to less expensive health insurance and generally better or more varied additional benefits; training resources; employee upkeep and current employee manuals vis workers' compensation; and the PEO will not tell the employer who to terminate, just how to do it."

Job descriptions for specific positions must be legally compliant, and aware of the ways to mitigate risk in hiring. While being an **equal opportunity employer** is a voluntary status, many want to qualify as such. An association may include in their compliance documents a written policy that they do not discriminate, and that they promote equal access for all employees.

It is required, however, that your job postings **comply with the ADA** (Americans with Disabilities Act), which prohibits discrimination against a qualified individual with a disability who can perform the essential functions of a job, with or without reasonable accommodation. It became fully effective in July 1994, and applies to employers with 15 employees or more. Understand the concept of **"reasonable accommodation**," which includes making facilities accessible and usable, restructuring or modifying jobs, acquiring or modifying equipment, and providing qualified readers and interpreters. If such "reasonable accommodation" of a disabled person requires "undue hardship" in terms of difficulty or expense, an organization may be exempt for such accommodation, under the ADA.

"Undue hardship" is evaluated in terms of the size of an organization, the type of its operations, and what it would cost to provide specific accommodations for an employee in a given position. A **disabled person** is someone with either a physical or mental impairment that substantially limits one or more major life activities; or has a record of such impairment which may include speech, sight, hearing or mental impairment, but may also pertain to HIV, diabetes, missing limbs, substance abuse recovery, or cancer survivor.

The ADA does not permit you to make pre-employment medical inquiries with the exception of drug testing. But once you make an offer to a candidate, you may require a medical exam so long as you have done the same to all other employees in that category.

The *Professional Practices in Association Management: The Essential Resource for Effective Management of Nonprofit Organizations* outlines the basic information that you should understand on the ADA guidelines pp 246-247.

Job descriptions provide evidence of each job's "essential functions"; the description can be used as the basis for discrimination, equal pay, and contract lawsuits. At minimum, a job description must list everything expected of someone doing a particular job; identify the major job functions or obligations from peripheral ones; offer a percentage of time to be spent at each function by way of indicating the relative importance of each one; specify the skills, physical demands, credentials and experience required to do each job; and identify which requirements are desired, preferred, or mandatory.

Technology systems sometimes seem like a moving target but the CSE must identify and implement such systems as are appropriate for your organization's needs and objectives as part of your **Technology administration,** and all aspects of managing or processing information in your association. This may involve bidding, purchasing, and maintaining your information technology systems, knowing what that entails, as well as the budgeting and recommendation of periodic upgrades.

Particularly with membership and financial databases, the CSE needs to ensure that your organization has secure technology systems, and must understand the components of privacy and access policies, procedures, and software. Developing and supervising a social media policy is also a knowledge area under your purview. But do remember: you are the Chief Staff Executive, **not** the chief Information or Technology Officer—be sure to make the distinction, and delegate.

That said, you do need to be on top of all technology trends, and how they impact the best practices of associations. These include social networks, blogs and eNewsletters, RSS feeds and Twitter. Out of each of these come both tools to analyze whether your technology infrastructure meets the needs and ambitions of your organization, and what policies for their use need to be in place.

Know the way to develop a **technology plan** that can then be approved by your board prior to implementation. Scan your association by setting goals, evaluating your needs for information technology, and understanding the trends. Then Plan, by matching systems that can meet those goals and support your needs; evaluate the security and back-up components of this technology, and calculate a timetable for installation or implementation. Implement by doing all of the contracts for software development or hardware purchase/rental; as you oversee that, understand how and by whom all necessary maintenance will be done. Finally, Evaluate your systems on a regular basis; there will invariably be updates or adjustments necessary.

For the CSE exam, it is recommended that you understand the five key steps to developing a **strategic technology process.** These involve forming a technology planning committee; conducting external and internal scans, including components of your association's operating strategic plan; evaluating various technology options as they pertain to your organization's goals; prioritizing any potential strategic technology initiatives; then implementing them following the steps identified above.

As with HR rules and regulations, the CSE is responsible for complying with all relevant laws that impact the association, and being aware of ways to mitigate the risk of failing to comply as part of your **Legal and Risk Management administration**. Oftentimes that involves soliciting the assistance of outside legal counsel, and knowing how to retain and manage legal aid. Internally, sometimes after they have been created or approved by outside counsel, CSEs should review and know how and when to use contracts, particularly with an eye to minimizing or mitigating the association's risk.

The **Legal and Risk Management** responsibilities tested on the exam also include knowing how to monitor all of an organization's actions and activities *vis á vis* your 501-c-3 or 501-c-6 non-profit status. This includes compliance with anti-trust laws. Associations tend to be susceptible to violations of them, such as: price setting, advertising prohibitions, requiring uniform terms, encouraging boycotting, suggesting specific raw materials, and profit levels. These are all potential **anti-trust**

violations, and you should have written guidelines to avoid such allegations. Share them with your chapters, staff, and leaders. The elements of a ***compliance program*** show that anti-trust behavior and conversations are not tolerated in your work environment. Demonstrating reasonable efforts to prevent such behavior goes a long way to protecting your association in court.

Know that the ***Federal Trade Commission Act*** gives the FTC the responsibility to prevent "Unfair methods of competition in or affecting commerce." The ***Robinson-Patman Act*** prohibits discriminatory pricing between purchasers of like commodities. The ***Clayton Act*** prohibits the restraint of trade through certain sorts of distribution activities, while the ***Sherman Act*** prohibits monopolies and other anti-competitive activities.

You should know what **corporate and governance documents** (like the corporate seal, bylaws, amendments, etc.) must be maintained and updated in order to conform to federal and state laws. There is a section devoted to this in the *Association*

Law Book, on the reading list. Study the relevant insurance coverage for associations, particularly **property & casualty,** which covers buildings and their contents plus "accidental bodily injury and personal injury or accidental property damage to another's property."

Also know the ways to protect your organization's fiduciary interests as well as that of the board, staff, and members. Most organizations have **intellectual property** now, as well. It is the general term for "intangible property that is the result of intellectual effort; is deemed to be unique and original; has marketplace value; and thus warrants protection under the law.

IP includes ideas; inventions, literary works, chemical business or computer processes, company names, and logos." It is discussed in detail in other domains, but there are four categories that you should understand: **copyright,** which is the "legal protection afforded an original work granting its owner the right to control it and prohibit others from using or profiting from it; **trademarks,** which is a "name, symbol, or other device that identifies a product, and is officially registered and legally restricted to the use by the owner or manufacturer," like company and product names, and logos; **patents** "for inventions and processes"; and **trade secrets** "for recipes, code and processes." Understand the ways in which you can protect IP, legally, through instruments like copyright, while ensuring its value and mitigating risk.

Know the distinction between **civil liability,** claims brought by individuals or companies due to personal injury; and **criminal liability,** wherein claims are brought by the government. In all matters of long-term contracting or other significant binding relationships, know the elements of **due diligence.** These may include fact, reference, and background checks; and assessing contractors or vendors *vis á vis* their ability to meet your requirements or their commitments. Due diligence as regards a partnership or merger may involve confirmation of an entity's finances, culture, and outstanding liabilities.

Sometimes there is also **personal liability** in your operations: claims are brought against staff, officers, or members of the board of directors of an organization. While rarely needed, it is considered essential to maintain ***Directors & Officers liability insurance*** that protects volunteers (and often the Executive Director, as well) from claims that arise from decisions made in good faith on behalf of the association. Some states allow organizations to indemnify their officers and directors except in criminal situations, or those involving gross negligence and fraud. Such indemnification should be stated in the association bylaws. **Ultra Vires** pertains to the involvement of directors, officers, and other volunteers in an association's activities beyond the corporate authority of the association. **Torts** are activities that cause injury or damage to persons or property.

The initial CSE responsibilities as regards **facilities management** are whether you **rent** (usually short-term; requires little capital but is the most expensive, in the long run); **lease** (most common, usually in 3-10-year contracts; allows you the option to negotiate for facilities improvements or renovations); or **own** your facility/office/building (gives you the best opportunity to budget for long-term expenses; offers you tax advantages like interest deductions and depreciation; gives you control and flexibility with your space, and the lowest long-term costs). Your management entails knowing how to evaluate your buildings and equipment in terms of your resource needs, and the financial obligations that attend to them.

As a facilities manager, you need to understand **OSHA's General Duty Clause,** and ensure that your workplace complies with all relevant regulations as regards its safety and accessibility. It needs to be free of any recognized hazards (unless you manage, say, a chemical plant that has its own OSHA regulations). In addition to your providing workers with a hazard-free workplace, you must also ensure that your employees comply with OSHA standards. Again, as mentioned above, if your association is larger than 15 employees, you must make reasonable accommodations under the ADA. Review what those are.

You must know how to put in place a crisis management program for your organization that protects all physical and human assets in the event of an emergency, and keeps them secure. Study the elements of **business continuity planning,** and know that the first goal is protecting the safety and welfare of your staff. After that, you need a plan for your association's property and data. There should be systems in place for communicating the emergence and response to any crisis first to your staff and board, then as relevant to your members or constituents and, in some cases, to the broader community. If you are a service provider, you need to plan ways to continue providing critical care or programs, and to restore critical services in the speediest manner possible.

You can use SPIE to develop your plan. But the components of your **plan** should be to plan for the crisis, establish policies, establish a command center, define then assess the crisis, determine the appropriate professional response, meet the needs of your logistics and human resources, then, once normality returns, review the components of your response, as a basis for future planning.

You and your team are also responsible for **vendor and supplier management.** This may be a major part of your association's activities and services, or may just be the outside printer and office supplies orders. In whatever aspect, you need to know how to evaluate the cost-benefit ratio and implications of keeping any of your association's services or functions in house as compared with outsourcing them. For larger purchases or contracts, you need to know how to establish requests for proposals (RFPs), and the elements of objective procedures around the RFP process to ensure that performance or proposals are evaluated fairly, and that vendors are selected without bias or any conflicts of interest. If your bylaws don't include policies regarding **conflict of interest** and **confidentiality**, you should work with your board to develop them along with documentation that ensures transparency in your association's dealing with vendors and suppliers.

Finally, the CSE exam covers general **business planning** in this domain, to some degree. You will want to review the ways that your organization's activities, programs, and business follow on the mission and strategic objectives of the association, as well as how they align with the available or obtainable resources. Retaining or obtaining legal, financial, and accounting services to provide protection and sustainability to your institution has been covered in other parts of the domains, but may be queried here, as well. You should know the elements of a **business plan** for any programs, services or products that an association has or plans to have; this includes an **operational plan**, and benchmarks for measuring outcomes. In association with a strategic plan, your business plan may be used for long-range funding development so that your capacity as CSE is not only to look just to the year ahead, but to manage your financial assets for a sustainable and adequate future.

I recommend that you read the Cox *Professional Practices in Association Management* chapters 5-6, 13-14, 16, 18, and 20 in order to prepare for the subject areas in this domain, along with the above-mentioned *Association Law Handbook,* chapters 2-5, 17, 24-26., and its 2009 update. Carol Barbieto's *Human Resource Policies and Procedures for Nonprofit Organizations* has not been updated in a number of years, but still includes valuable fundamentals, if HR is not your general background as CAE. *Core Competencies in Association Professional Development* on the reading list devotes chapter 11 to Management, Staffing, and Administration, while *The Volunteer Management Handbook* chapters 3 and 4 look at HR considerations as regards volunteers, and *The Jossey-Bass Handbook* chapters 22-25 cover the recruitment and retention of great people.

CHAPTER 7

DOMAIN 4: KNOWLEDGE MANAGEMENT & RESEARCH

This domain currently covers between 4-6% of the CSE examination. **Knowledge management** is the sharing, capturing and using of institutional knowledge to provide services to your constituents. It involves developing strategies to create, safeguard, and use the knowledge assets in your organization so that the right information flows to the right people and at the right time in order to use these assets to create value.

Managing these assets well helps your association to better organize and utilize knowledge, reduce staff time looking for information, ensure less work duplication and better customer service, and return to your organization more time to improve member services. You are required to be able to identify the diverse information needs and preferences of an association's membership and other stakeholders, and then to develop appropriate knowledge management programs that disseminate intellectual and knowledge-based assets.

Know the difference between **data** (just raw information: numbers, dates, letters), **information** (which is meaning through connection; data together in sentences or conveying something relevant), and **knowledge** (applied information; answers the question, 'how?'). There are two types of knowledge: **explicit** knowledge can be explained or articulated by individuals in an organization; **tacit** is the sort that remains in the heads of individuals in the association. **Knowledge management** can be viewed as a cyclical process wherein first you identify what knowledge exists in your organization and where; then design methods for knowledge exchange;

integrate your knowledge into the operations of your organization; and disseminate or share it.

You should see knowledge as one of your strategic business goals, and help to design systems so that it is embedded into everything that you and your staff do. You need to make the connection between what is explicit and implicit within your own institution, and figure out how to transmit your knowledge management program in order to share cutting-edge professional or industry learning, insights, and best practices. Success is defined as creating context, continuity, meaning, and value for your members. Internally, you want to evaluate how your knowledge management impacts the leadership within your association, your institutional culture, the roles and responsibilities of your board and staff, and your technology infrastructure.

Abstract and information management systems facilitate collaborative online database management for use in membership management, conferences and meeting management, and financials. Know about **communities of practice,**

informal networks and forums where knowledge is exchanged and generated; and groups of professionals bound by common problems or the pursuit of solutions that then lead them to embody knowledge.

For the exam, the **eight core Knowledge Management tasks** of a CSE are to identify diverse information needs; develop and manage your KM program; serve the information needs of your stakeholders; share through utilizing your KM system; deliver high-quality services and products; review and repackage information efficiently; evaluate your KM services on an ongoing basis; and support continuous improvement.

As part of this domain, you are responsible for understanding how to develop a **research agenda** for your association that assists you, internally, while it helps to advance your industry or field, and then provides necessary information to your members or stakeholders. You need to know about **evaluation** methods so that you can use your research and collected data in order to guide your operations and planning decisions. This includes the basics of **statistics,** and the elements of customized research reports that may be needed to meet the interests or needs of your constituency. Although mentioned elsewhere, you also need to know how to develop a customized data reporting system that helps you and your board develop strategy and positioning.

Research is best designed from a place of "why" you need information about a given project or direction, as the answer is not just "to benefit your members," which is a big general reason for doing things, but more specifically "why" you need to know details on a specific program. In order to develop an effective **research agenda**, you first identify the objectives of your research, and then look to the quality of answers you need. This process will lead you to the questions you want to pose. Is what you need to know available anywhere else? Say, at the Answer Bureau or Department of Labor?

Then, what sort of research do you need to do? **Primary research** is original and oftentimes expensive, but provides you with new data around a select issue or concern. It should have clear objectives, and recognize nuance. **Secondary research** is based upon data that were compiled by others and then either interpreted by the original researcher or by your association. It could include statistics from outside firms, materials from the library, government reports, trade articles, etc. that was accumulated for reasons other than yours and your association's, but which could illuminate a question or concern that you have. **Internal research** (like a survey of member needs) is different than **external** (such as a compensation study).

You may need to do a **market analysis,** which looks at costs, trends, competitors, etc. Alongside that you may do research on **operating ratios**, as a means of comparison with competitors or comparable organizations. You may need the information from **compensation surveys** (and this is an example of research that may have been done already, for your sector). **Benchmarking** is a type of research for best practices. If you are doing

summative evaluation, it examines something once it is over, such as the evaluation of a seminar or workshop by participants once they complete it. **Formative evaluations** are research used "to shape" something, whether planning or programming; it might be a survey of needs or desires that provides data used in your programmatic planning for a coming year or conference.

Methodologies for data collection in **member research** include *surveys*, either paper or electronic; these help to tell you demographic information about your membership, and to gather feedback on your services, programs, or priorities. When you are doing *exploratory research*, you may be well served to compose some *focus groups*. Qualitative data can be gathered electronically, but also through *telephone interviews* if you design closed-ended questions that are clear and consistent. *Personal interviews*, on the other hand, permit you to be more flexible, and to clarify contradictions or confusions; you must ensure against bias in your sample, to be sure that it is representative of your broader constituency or market. Study a comparison of the relative costs, time, response rates, and sample validity of the various research techniques. *Professional Practices in Association Management* offers one on p. 214.

You also need to evaluate the statistical accuracy of your research sample, and the difference between **stratified sampling,** where your samples segments are divided into groups, as compared with **quota sampling,** the number of people you want surveyed. As regards **quality control,** know both what the **confidence level** is—a measure of how representative your sample is of a total population; and **level of error,** the variation in responses between the sample and the total (sometimes called the deviation).

Know the **80-20 rule** or **Pareto Principle,** that states that, in many events, roughly 80% of the effects come from 20% of the causes, or 80% of your sales come from 20% of your clients, etc. Understand numerical summaries: **mean/average** is the sum of all numbers divided by the number of observations;

median is the middle, or the number in the middle of a set of numbers ranked from high to low; and **mode,** which is the number that appears most frequently in a set of numbers.

Once you have your data and research, you will also want to know about the **methods of reporting** that information. Typical report formats are *written*, either printed, PDF, or on your website where you can share the greatest amount of detail; *data tables,* which are often useful to share and make adjustments between managers or committee members with updates, projections, etc.; and an *interactive database,* sometimes housed on a website or in a CD, which can be very customized.

Be aware that there are antitrust and anti-competition issues that may be raised around your research, so know **the law** as it pertains to your project, in order to protect your association, legally. Participation has to be voluntary, and your research must have a purpose of collecting useful business data, not affecting competitors' agreements. Data needs to be about the past, not projected into the future. Individuals' data should remain confidential, and presented only in aggregate form. Don't share one respondent's data with any other survey participant. Don't include recommendations in the published report, and make the report available to non-members if they have a reasonable need for the conclusions.

You may charge non-members for your reports, but not so much that they are forced to become members. You are allowed to restrict the sharing of your results to participants only; in that case, non-members as well as non-participants would not have access to your data or conclusions.

I recommend that you look at chapters 18 and 19 of Cox's *Professional Practices in Association Management* to supplement your study for this domain, as well as Tracey and Edwards' *Core Competencies in Association Professional Development*. There are a few helpful tips regarding the anti-trust laws as they pertain to association research in the *Association Law Handbook*.

Association Management Excellence

CHAPTER 8

DOMAIN 5: GOVERNANCE AND STRUCTURE

The fifth subject area on the CAE examination evaluates your understanding of the corporate and governing structure that is unique to American not-for-profit organizations, and will comprise 9-11% of your test. It starts with the very definition of an "association," and how to establish and maintain an effective and representative system to govern an organization in order to ensure that it delivers on its organizing principles and stated mission. This may involve establishing management units like committees, special interest groups, sections or task forces in order to develop or effectuate your association's mission.

An **association** is "a group of individuals, sharing common interests and goals, who collectively accomplish what they could not accomplish alone." There are a number of types of associations. **Trade associations** are organized under section 501-c-6 of the tax code; they are a group of individuals and/or companies that are concerned with a specific type of field or business, or the services or products related to same; they cannot solicit funds from the general public, but are free to engage in unlimited legislative activity provided that does not involve political activity.

Professional associations or societies are comprised of people with experience or knowledge that qualifies them as specialists, or they share a field of practice or business within a profession; they may have a specific credential.

501-c-3s must be "charitable, educational, scientific or literary as their predominant focus," (80-95% devoted to one or more exempt public purpose) and can solicit tax-deductible funds from the general public; they may not allocate any significant part of their budget or activities to propaganda or legislative influence, nor may they engage in any political campaigns. **501-c-4s** must devote over half of their activities to social welfare, and may participate in lobbying and political activity if directed at such social welfare. Know the criteria to qualify and the limitations of each type of tax-exempt status.

Some organizations are **volunteer-driven,** which is to say that volunteers "make the basic decisions about the direction of the association and allocation of resources; have veto power over programming decisions, and have direct impact on budgeting decisions." Other associations are **staff-driven,** where staff makes the budgeting and programming decisions, while volunteers have an advisory capacity and little day-to-day impact; volunteers focus on strategic, long-range and policy issues. The **balanced mode** has "staff responsible for day-to-day operational-related matters, and volunteers responsible for governance and other member-related matters."

In the event that an association incorporates a subsidiary in order to do for-profit business related to or funding the non-profit, that new entity must be incorporated as either a **C-Corp** (commercial corporation) or as an **S-Corp** (service corporation). There are differences between them, and these are identified in their Articles of Incorporation papers. For example, C-Corps can have many classes of stock and an unlimited number of shareholder/owners. S-Corps are limited to 75 shareholders who must be US citizens, and accept a single class of stock.

Associations may organize into any one of a number of types of organizations. A **federation** is composed of other associations with a common interest. A **horizontal** association serves only one functional level of a profession or industry. **Vertical** organizations encompass all of the functional areas of a profession or occupation, like all of the CSEs in your state, for example.

Two-tiered associations permit both state and local chapters to join a national organization, while **three-tiered** has the local chapters join a state association, and the state organization affiliates with the national entity. **Reciprocal or Unified** associations provide for an automatic set of privileges with another organization as a benefit of membership, while **contingent** organizations require that members join both an association and its local chapter. **Conglomerate or combination** associations include a mix of individual and corporate members.

The association is managed by a volunteer **Board of Directors** that is responsible for **governance**—that is, "what" the organization should achieve without any legal or ethical compromise. There is an ideal separation of duties between the board of directors, which should address broad policy issues related to direction, strategy, and results; and the **Executive committee,** which can build the board agenda through considering issues in collaboration with the CSE. The **Chief Staff Executive** is responsible for all operational and staff issues, while the **board chair** should manage the governance workforce. **Transparency,** which is operating in an open, accountable manner that shares useful information to the public for organizational evaluation, is considered a best practice.

There are some absolutes to know as regards the **best practices for governance** of a modern association. This initial separation of duties between Board and Staff are at the foundation. When problems arise with volunteers like the Board members, volunteers should handle those issues, while the CSE manages the staff. The ASAE advises that the CSE maintain the distinction between governance (Board) and operations (staff) as the volunteer Board members will be more responsive to one another than to a CSE, even though she/he is the chief employee of the association.

The CSE is never the peer of a Board member, but serves as a liaison with the Board and Executive committee in order to implement the Board's policy and vision. CSEs need to know how to facilitate the activities of all of the many governing units within the organization.

Additional absolutes as regards the governance of an organization include the facts that the Board must be confidential, obey all laws, speak with only <u>one</u> voice, and only through actions or positions that have been agreed upon. The Board should represent or maintain a clear connection to the "owners" of an association—these include members and funders. Their responsibilities include assuring organizational performance, creating policies for the CSE to implement and act (freely, ethically, and legally), and adopting visionary outcomes. Only the CSE reports directly to a Board, and only the CSE is responsible for the institutional performance and operations. All other paid staff, contractors, and volunteers must report only to the CSE.

High impact Boards have a clear and detailed strategic framework; a formal design for the board's governing work; standing committees that provide effective governance; a disciplined self-management that includes accountability; and strong CSE support.

They often determine their own budget just for governance, which includes allocations for their training (either in-house, or attending workshops); the financial and maybe a compliance audit or other third-party analyses of the association's performance; surveys, opinion polls, and meeting costs; and a budget for staff support to the activities of the Board. This goes a long way to telling the CSE what the Board requires for expenditures, when the CSE begins work on the association budget.

Ensure that you know the rules for handling Board meeting **minutes,** which must only record motions, votes, and assignments, never references to who said what. Recognize that over-detailed minutes may jeopardize the association. Where non-controversial or routine items can be read in advance and batched together and approved in a single motion, a **consent agenda** can improve meeting efficiency. All items like committee reports, etc., need to be in writing and circulated for inclusion; individual items may be withdrawn from the agenda whenever any board member so requests.

Know the elements of *Robert's Rules of Order* as regards the standard procedures for a governing body to conduct business in an orderly fashion. In some instances, associations or their committees adopt a **consensus model** wherein decision-making requires agreement by all of the members of a group, rather than just a majority. Be aware of new technologies for taking and approving minutes. Also be aware that some board meeting issues may require **dialogue before deliberation,** wherein they are discussed with members at large and the findings are brought in for inclusion in the board conversation or vote.

Other documents that are mandatory for associations are:

1. **Articles of Incorporation,** which is an agreement between the association and the state, and should be short;
2. **Bylaws** or the Association Constitution, which is an agreement between the Board of Directors and members, and may be amended as the organization grows or changes;

3. **Policies,** the parameters or mandates set by the Board. If a Policy manual exists, that is the third most important legal organizational document, followed by meeting minutes;
4. **Procedures,** as defined above—the step-by-step processes of how tasks are accomplished within a given association; these are operational, however, and not "governing documents";
5. **Practices,** which are the way things are done within a given organization, but that aren't documented above.

CSEs need to know how to align all of the governance documents, and keep them that way.

Committees are units of organization that often determine the "how" to do or to implement the "what" established by the Board of Directors. They often work with staff. Know the differences between **standing committees** (ones that perform an on-going function, like the nominating committee; identified within an organization's bylaws)**, Ad Hoc committees** (special committees established around a specific problem or task, then disbanded), **and Task Forces** (a special committee given a defined time requirement).

The **audit committee** is another standing committee, and should define the scope of the organization's audit, review proposals and recommend an outside firm for the full Board's approval. Auditing is a Board function; budget development is not, as it is operational, although the Board should establish policies that address budget parameters. The CSE should not hire the audit firm, as doing so poses a conflict of interest.

Remember that you are subject to **Sarbanes-Oxley,** the "Public Company Accounting Reform and Investor Protection Act" (in the Senate) and the "Corporate and Auditing Accountability and Responsibility Act" (in the House), a federal law that set new or enhanced standards for all U.S. public company boards, management and public accounting firms. It has provisions that require that there be members of your Audit committee that have financial expertise; that your association contract with registered auditors; and that certified financial statements are advised. Finance committees as standing committees are becoming less prevalent; they are being replaced by staff CFOs.

Special interest groups operate with a limited amount of autonomy, but may have jurisdiction over an area or interest. Within associations, they may be **membership sections,** although membership sections are usually more permanent than SIGs. There is an additional meaning in politics which refers to PACs, and legislative or electoral influence.

The recruitment and development of volunteer managers is included in this domain. You should know how to establish a volunteer recruitment and training program that establishes the skills or qualifications necessary, as well as clear lines of action as to who is responsible for doing what, by when, and for what cost. **Orientation** for board members and other volunteers needs to include ethical and fiduciary responsibilities so that management and governance are done correctly, and protects the organization from risk.

Confidentiality is "one of the key duties related to fiduciary responsibility of a governing body; maintaining confidentiality on sensitive issues fulfills the legal duty of loyalty to the organization."

To inform their legal orientation, provide all new board members with the association's Articles of Incorporation and most current Bylaws. For their orientation to management, provide a description of all of the positions, and an organizational chart where available. Include the most recent Strategic Plan, copies of meeting minutes for the past two years, the current operating budget and most recent audit report, and any key contracts. Other internal documents that should be provided include any standing Code of Ethics, and documentation of the difference between strategic governance and operational management.

Volunteer management incorporates strategies for engagement and retention—a volunteer may not remember when you say "thank you," but always recalls when you have not. The CSE must clarify the commitment and expectations for all volunteers, including meeting attendance and responsibilities or charges.

The elements of a defined **volunteer leadership development** plan include criteria for specific leadership positions, volunteer job descriptions, defined leadership training, successor management, and a system for evaluation/feedback. Structures for accountability are imperative, and serve to engage and retain active volunteer members. **Succession planning** is a critical part of governance on both the volunteer leadership level as well as for top staff.

Component relations will also be tested in this domain. You must know how to establish the procedures and policies that form affiliates or chapters; these charters need to include policies, formation guidelines like affiliation agreements and standards of affiliation. An **affiliation agreement** is any partnership or memorandum of understanding between the national or parent association and its chapters or affiliates; it should include descriptions of how each component should be governed, and should bind the organizations together.

A national organization must design mechanisms for maintaining control over local or regional affiliates; in particular, they need to control local membership requirements to ensure that there are no violations of antitrust laws. Know how to use **charter agreements** to define all of the critical lines of responsibility and authority, and also how to ensure the success of any association components or their activities.

Affiliates need to have clearly defined boundaries, and a clear grievance procedure in order to be effective partners in realizing or delivering on your association's mission. The more transparency you can create with your chapters or components, the more successful that relationship. **Open communication channels** are used to exchange relevant and correct information between the parent association and its components or members. These may include email, newsletters, teleconferences, national conferences, in-person visits by staff to affiliates or by regional leaders to headquarters, and, social networks. Be certain to solicit input from your affiliates before establishing a new program or service. Having them on board will make any launch all the more effective.

Design mechanisms for **resolving conflicts** that arise in affiliate relations and that ensure that a CSE can maintain objectivity. Require that each party in disagreement write two pages that represent their side of an issue. Convene a three-person review board to determine who has primary responsibility for the issue, and ensure that they lead the process for determining a solution.

There is a lot of outside material available for review on governance and structure. I recommend that you look at chapters 1, 7 and 8 in the *Professional Practices in Association Management;* review chapters 1-29 in the *Association Law Handbook*, plus with chapters 51, 62 and 81. *The Volunteer Management Handbook* is uniquely written to assist in your studying for this domain, while chapters 3-7 in *the Jossey-Bass Handbook* should also be read or reviewed.

CHAPTER 9

DOMAIN 6: PUBLIC POLICY, GOVERNMENT RELATIONS, AND COALITION BUILDING

6-8% of your CSE exam will include questions that relate to public policy and government relations. The rules that apply to an association's engagement with public policy on the federal level will be on the exam. **Public Policy** pertains broadly to activities and interests that are focused on relevant initiatives of the government and "the public sector." **Government relations** covers a span of activities between governmental and non-governmental entities that could be merely relationship building or monitoring, or could involve direct partnerships or lobbying.

GR activities may include hiring a **lobbyist,** a person or firm "employed or retained for financial or other compensation to make more than one lobbying contact, and who must be registered with the federal or state governments where such contacts are made." GR may also involve influencing an issue, holding a conference for legislators or inviting them to do a site visit, monitoring regulations or legislation on various issues of concern, or organizing grassroots lobbying (see below). By contrast, **external relations** involves building a relationship between your association and any other non-governmental person/organization, like universities, think tanks and foundations, or other associations that share your concerns and may be built into an effective **coalition,** or alliance for public relations or lobbying purposes.

The ways that a CSE should approach public policy begin with being able to identify and analyze an association's need to engage in activities that develop or impact public policy. Next, you should know how to identify and foster advocacy sources that already support your industry. **Advocacy** involves attempting to influence a decision-maker or decision–making entity on some issue that is important to your association. For your purposes, it involves influencing legislation or moving the public to act in some way beneficial for your organization or some aspect of its mission. You may find it useful to create or sponsor advocacy programs.

Government relations programs that are planned, implemented, then evaluated by the CSE must follow policies that have been approved by your board. Formal procedures often include input from your association membership, and may best be developed in a Government Relations committee of your board if your association plans to be engaged in GR to a serious degree.

You will need to know how to monitor legislation and regulations on the state and local level, along with federal laws or initiatives. Part of your public policy agenda should include reports to membership and other stakeholders that educates them on the issues germane to your industry and mission, and where specific legislation is involved, how and who to contact in order to add support to your advocacy agenda.

Non-lobbying activities include published or disseminated public communications; requests for information; providing testimony before congressional committees if requested; legally confidential communications to the government; communications on behalf of foreign parties or governments; written responses to official requests for information; and any communications made in public proceedings or judicial adjudications, on the record.

Where your association is legally permitted to undertake lobbying activities, you need to know how to identify and retain registered lobbyists, as well as how to monitor and engage with them. **Lobbying** is any written or oral communication with some government elected or staff official, including congresspersons, their aides or staff, members of the

President's cabinet or their offices, and other political appointees. **501-c-3s** may lobby if they spend less than five percent (5%) of their operating budget on the task, but *absolutely prohibited from participating in political campaigns to support or oppose candidates for public office. (*Very serious.)*

Reporting may be done either through the "**no substantial part**" test which limits 501-c-3s to lobbying "an insubstantial amount," which has not been defined by the IRS per se, so courts suggest that 5% is "insubstantial"; or the "**expenditure**" test by 501(h) election for 501-c-6 organizations, which is more clearly defined as to what is and isn't lobbying, and sets clear $1 million expenditure limits and calculations. The penalty for violating either test or for exceeding their limits, is the loss of tax-exempt status.

According to the **De Minimus rule,** you may consider any staff member's time spent lobbying as 0 if less than 5% of their time is spent doing so, unless it is direct contact lobbying. **501-h-**electing organizations under the federal tax code have a "sliding scale of permissible lobbying amounts for direct and grassroots lobbying" of 20% or less over a four-year period.

Direct lobbying involves contacting a lawmaker regarding a specific position on a piece of legislation. **Grassroots lobbying,** by contrast, is a way to influence legislation through the organization of public sentiment, and *their* communication with representatives (via email, calls, petitions, etc.). A CSE should know how to evaluate whether some sort of grassroots activity would be influential in a cause, and how to implement this sort of lobbying.

Lobbying contact is the oral or written communication; **lobbying activities** are actions that support that contact. Just providing information to your members about bills is not considered lobbying, unless your "association has evidenced a purpose to influence legislation;" once you do, however, all actions and their costs are considered lobbying, and must be accounted for as such.

The **Omnibus Budget Reconciliation of 1993** "imposes significant recordkeeping requirements and administrative burdens on associations." Know that it eliminated your ability to deduct the expense of lobbying on your business tax returns; it also requires associations to notify their members about what portion of their dues is attributed to lobbying, as it is then not tax-deductible, either. It provides an alternative to that, which is to pay a 35% **proxy tax** (like an excise tax on your lobbying expenditures).

You may use a "reasonable method" to allocate your costs between activities, including lobbying, which means that it must be consistent. The **estimation rule** requires lobbying organizations to notify their membership about that percentage of their dues that goes to lobbying. The **allocation rule** says "lobbying associations must allocate on a dollar-for-dollar basis, all expenditures for federal and state lobbying against dues and similar income received by the association."

There are four ways to calculate your lobbying expense. **The ratio method** multiplies your total cost of operations by "lobbying hours divided by total labor hours, then add the result to any third-party lobbying costs." **The gross up method** multiplies your basic labor costs for lobbying (wages or other costs of labor including third-party costs) times 175%. The **alternative gross-up method** includes no hours for your support staff, but you multiply the cost of all other lobbying wages times 225%. The **section 273a method** combines the gross-up and ratio method, even if you have volunteers that conduct some lobbying activities.

In some instances, it may be advisable for your association to establish a **political action committee (PAC).** Know that a 501-c-6 may start a PAC, and use your association funds to pay for the administration and solicitation expenses of a PAC, but you can't contribute those funds to the PAC. 501-c-3s cannot have a PAC. PACs must register with the FEC within 10 days after they are formed, and both receipts and disbursements have to be reported every quarter (more often after state and federal elections). All of the most current details are available at the FEC website at www.FEC.gov. Membership associations can solicit their members and families to make contributions to a PAC, but trade associations need corporate permission.

Individual cash contribution limits to a PAC are $100, and $5,000 total per year; while there is no **limit for corporations,** although they have to give you approval in order to solicit their employees, and "each member corporation can approve solicitation by only one federal PAC per year," and members, families, and staff can only be solicited twice each year. Even without approval, a PAC may "maintain a booth at meetings, provided there is no publicity."

For the CAE examination, be certain to know all federal laws that affect association lobbying. Have good clear definitions for terms related to GR. Memorize all relevant quantifiable requirements—all of the dollar limitations, filing deadlines, and easily testable numbers related to federal regulations of non-profit government relations, like the "annual individual limit for contributions to an association PAC is $5,000," or "PACs must be registered within

10 days following their formation." Review all of the key regulators and regulatory requirements for lobbying associations.

As regards the **internal revenue service (IRS),** know the differences between 501-c-3 and 501-c-6 corporations, and all IRS requirements for nonprofits that engage in lobbying activities. Review precisely how the IRS defines lobbying and non-lobbying activities.

As regards Congressional rules and reporting, review the Federal Lobbying Disclosure Act (LDA of 1995), and the Honest Leadership and Open Government Act of 2007 (HLOGA) which amended it, at the website (you can find it at http://lobbyingdisclosure.house.gov), plus any new regulations mentioned in the *Law Review 2009 Update.* The HLOGA created more stringent registration and reporting requirements of lobbyists, restricted gifts to legislators including meals, and created tougher penalties for failures to comply. It requires quarterly lobbying reports on the 20th of April, July, October and January; lobbying firms with incomes over $2,500 and associations with expenses greater than $10,000 that employ an in-house lobbyist must report each quarter; and registered lobbyists must report by Jan 30 and July 30 each year on all of their expenses, including all campaign contributions and event costs, plus certify that they followed House and Senate rules *vis á vis* travel and gifts.

HLOGA requires that affiliated entities who support and control lobbying activities have to disclose any donors, members, or sponsors that contribute over $5,000/quarter. Lobbyists must disclose any past government service going back twenty (20) years. All reports must be filed electronically, Congresspersons and their staff cannot accept any gifts or travel costs, and the criminal and civil penalties for violations were increased to up to $200,000 in fines and 5 years in prison.

The **Federal Election Committee (FEC)** defines the rules for PACs, election laws, reporting schedules, and campaign contributions.

Be sure that you understand the strategies for developing an effective Government Relations plan so that it is an effective relationship-building process that involves planning, elections, relationships, and expertise in both issues/subjects of importance to your association, as well as expertise in the levers and mechanisms of government. Know how to prioritize your stakeholders' key advocacy issues, then build leadership including possibly a GR committee with board and general members.

Keep your members educated about policy matters that affect your association and its priorities, and communicate the value of lobby activities to them on a regular basis as part of their ROI. Make legislative developments and issues part of your member communication and annual gatherings or meetings, maximizing the capacity of your technology and information systems to inform or organize your constituents around key action items. And know that there is always strength in numbers, so build Coalitions with other associations and share resources to communicate your concerns.

Coalition building is the third component of this domain, and it involves identifying and bringing together other groups that share the interests of your association to obtain mutual goals through activities done together. These may be short-term or long-term coalitions; they may organize around a single matter that is addressed in a specific time period, or may focus on ongoing efforts. Understand how to forge a coalition-building model that can respond to the needs of your stakeholders, and be flexible enough to umbrella various other associations and interest groups. Whether formal or informal, the relationships can be highly beneficial: know how to communicate the potential values in coming and working together. Consider the various ways that groups may work together, including partnerships and alliances.

Sometimes coalitions can be effective in **issues management,** which is a PR campaign focused on a regulation or piece of legislation, and which would benefit from your influencing or controlling public opinion. Whether alone as an association or with others, issues management involves defining the goal (for example, the passage or blocking of a bill); forging a message; selecting key influencers and opinion makers; developing a message campaign to reach those audiences; charting the success or momentum of that messaging; then responding to public perception. Clarity and consistent focus are of paramount importance at all stages.

On the reading list, Amy Showalter's *Creating and Managing an Association Government Relations Program* is essential for review in this subject area, along with chapters 40-50 of the *Association Law Handbook* and chapters 1, 21-22 and 24 in the *Professional Practices in Association Management*. Chapter 10 in *The Jossey-Bass Handbook* addresses non-profit lobbying. There are also a lot of resources available from the ASAE on Government Relations, plus classes offered in Washington, DC.

CHAPTER 10

DOMAIN 7: MEMBERSHIP DEVELOPMENT

Many associations have members, so it is no surprise that membership development constitutes 10-12% of the CAE examination. Each organization and its CSE must know how to look at the value offered each one of its members strategically, and know how to communicate their return on investment (ROI) for joining your association.

The first part of this knowledge area involves the management of **member relations.** Your ability to retain a member begins with the point of first contact between that individual and your association. An initial portion of the CSE's responsibilities *vis á vis* members involves strategically positioning your members and potential members in relation to government, media, and public affairs. Through your association's attitudes and opinions, communicated through **public relations,** your objective is to move people closer to your organization and its work.

Your Board and active volunteers are the conduit for defining expectations and for communicating the mission, priorities, and activities of the association that will keep members engaged and informed. The CSE must design and implement communication strategies on various platforms and registers, in order to deliver these messages. Sometimes the Board and volunteers need training to support this function.

Public opinion is managed by the CSE first of all because it speaks to a broad pool of **prospective members.** Study public relations concepts that pertain to member relations, like the **spiral of silence, predisposition, perception, and cognitive dissonance.** Know how to incorporate research and diversity in order to "integrate the context and cultural norms of potential members into an association's outreach efforts." Identify the types of activities and opportunities that will permit member contributions to your association's progress. These may be focused, short-term opportunities, rotating committee participation, or significant leadership roles accompanied by leadership development organized by the CSE.

Examine innovative ways that you can communicate with your members, including the various delivery methods for member messaging, and the ways to target specific audiences depending upon the message that you have to relay. Know how to establish industry awards or member recognition programs that might help your association with its profile and other goals, as well as engage volunteers.

Define your association's **privacy policy**, or study examples that you encounter everywhere, like the one at the IEEE (http://goo.gl/53uWDc). You are responsible for ensuring that staff and members comply with all privacy provisions.

Building your membership through recruitment, then retaining your members through effective management are additional responsibilities of the CSE. Know the differences between an association having **membership categories,** which are defined in the bylaws, and stand in relation to regular members; **membership classes,** which is a type of designation that accords various privileges, and which includes regular, life member, associate or student members, honorary, etc.; and a **membership section,** which focuses on defined interests under the umbrella of a profession, and which may have independent professional development or services that involve those interests.

Membership dues structure is the entire framework for assessing dues on your membership. It includes a **dues base,** which describes the "units or entities on which dues are measured e.g., sales volume, or flat rate." It includes the **dues rate,** which is the amount assessed annually, although it may be done on a **sliding scale,** where your dues rate decreases the more your dues base grows. The dues structure also identifies the way a member calculates what they owe the association.

Certain sorts of **membership restrictions** are not permitted; this and various fees are leading to some organizations having anti-trust and other legal issues. Know that your association may not require that members retain a certain amount of stock in a trade; may not create any geographical boundary that limits where members may serve; and may not limit membership. Members cannot be permitted to deny or block prospective members, and associations may not limit or cap membership, nor grant some member exclusive rights to operate in a given area.

Reasonable membership restrictions *are* permitted. For example, you may limit membership to a profession or trade, to professionals engaged at a certain level of function or responsibility, and those willing to abide by a certain ethical code. You can require that members pay dues promptly, and you can have **reasonable qualifications.** These may include certain minimum sizes of businesses, sales, or output; a minimum percentage of business within a specific profession; educational or achievement prerequisites, and membership conditioned on membership in another association.

The laws pertaining to membership classes and restrictions, along with issues around fees and pricing are available in the *Association Law Handbook,* pp. 246, 253, 263 and 280. Know about the legal requirements for expulsion or membership termination, as well. Jacobs covers that on p. 257, but know that your association had to have reasonable standards for expulsion and fair procedures for membership termination within legal guidelines.

You are permitted to expel a member who willfully violates the association's code of ethics, fails to pay dues, no longer meets the membership definition in your bylaws, and receives 2/3 vote of the Board for cause. You should have a process that includes a notice that you intend to proceed against this individual; a recitation of any accusation, failing, or charges; notice for a fair hearing on the matter; opportunity for the charged individual to examine any evidence or question any witnesses; the opportunity to refute all charges; and the right to counsel where applicable.

The first watchword in membership recruitment is that it is all about the **perceived value** of joining your association or cause; not the product. Retention should start with a needs analysis of your members **and prospects,** so know how to design a **Needs Analysis** of your audience, what content that will involve and which logistics. Know how to do pilot testing, and how to integrate your analysis into other services and programs, plus any legal issues involved with this assessment.

Once you complete this critical research, you should know how to develop a recruitment marketing plan in association with your current Strategic Plan. Study a sample membership plan at Gin Comm Group's website, www.gincomm.com.

Be aware of the idea of **golden handcuffs** as it pertains to member services. This is a product or service that "builds loyalty because it is unattainable elsewhere." While these may assist in recruitment and retention, and become tent poles of an association's sales pitch, know that most every service or product can be duplicated by a competitor or for-profit corporation; this can degrade the reliability of income or membership based on your handcuffs.

Recognize that your marketing strategy must be personalized and customized, and needs to empathize with your audience. No one approach will suit all of your prospective members, so you need to identify the *type of prospect, what you need to know about them,* and *how you can help them.* Highlight the product or service that your association offers that is unique: it can't be purchased elsewhere, so your organization is *the place to be.* Know how to highlight and expand upon a member's ROI. There are various types of target marketing strategies, some more effective than others. They include working trade shows, holding conventions, MGAM (member get a member, which is not very effective), DM and others.

Dr. Dale Paulsen writes clearly about membership marketing in his blog at www.ytheyjoin.com, which is worth review; he also publishes articles about target marketing at www.EZineArticles.com. He identifies nine types of members based on their "professional needs and motivations rather than traditional demographics and they include: Mailboxer; Relevant Participant; Shaper; CompShopper; Cognoscenti; Booster; Altruistic; Doubter; and Non-Relevant." This analysis is very informative, and served as a precursor to the segmented, long-tail, and social media marketing that has evolved today.

Be able to use analytic tools to evaluate the satisfaction of your membership, along with trends in your membership's needs and demographics so that you can assess the relevance of your services and programs on an ongoing basis.

Membership is often affected by external trends, be they economic, social, cultural, and global, as many associations noted during the financial crisis of 2009. *Professional Practices in Association Management* identifies the potential macros v. micro levers that you should know on p. 373, along with the impacts of regional economies.

Some associations are international, or can benefit from an international **strategic alliance,** which is a long-term commitment that involves "shared or transferred decision-making and a formal agreement." These alliances can be of benefit because they often involved a consolidation of administration, and shared programming. They do not change your corporate structure, however.

The ASAE recommends strategic alliances because they can assist associations in "creating efficiencies, outreach, program or geographic expansion," and may lead to a merger or corporate integration. *Professional Practices in Association Management* discusses alliances, as well as international partnerships and relationships, along with the elements of an **MOU (Memorandum of Understanding)** and an **SOU (Statement of Understanding)** on p. 375.

A **globalization strategy** involves establishing international chapters, securing local access so that you either hold meetings or provide services in international regions, and finding partners in other associations internationally. It requires **global localization** to identify the individual needs and wants of any given region, plus an investigation into what laws, regulations and ethical standards apply to your association's work.

An **international association** has a "significant portion of membership based outside one region, or members headquartered in one region with significant interests in other regions." A **global association** has "direct membership spread over two or more regions of the world, more or less equally, and no one country holds a Board majority."

The membership domain also holds you responsible for knowing about how to create an environment within your organization where members adhere to high ethical standards. Know how to formulate an **ethics program** that establishes and enforces standards of ethical behavior, including education programs that help your members comply with the association's standards. Your ethics and self-regulation programs should examine and measure the association's conduct, and ensure that everyone involved follows the appropriate processes, and legal and ethical business practices.

Ethics and self-regulation procedures are expected throughout an association. Know the elements of building a documented process that develops and maintains your program, along with the elements of an environment that cultivates and expects high standards. Include procedures for educating your membership, and that assign detailed responsibilities to volunteer leadership and to staff.

A **code of ethics** should request or require members to adhere to "minimum standards of practices and policies." It should include a procedure for administering sanctions that should include written notice, a hearing, the right to appeal, the avoidance of anger, and the avoidance of a "competitive motive or conflict of interest among staff and volunteers participating in the enforcement of the Code."

Self-regulation programs are not mandated by the government; they comprise "a regulatory process in which the trade or professional association sets and enforces rules and standards relating to the conduct of firms/individuals in the industry *in lieu of* government regulation." This contrasts with government-based programs like accreditation, licensing, and defined standards for products or services.

Know that you must be mindful of anti-trust problems when creating a self-regulation program. You **should not** suggest profit levels, set prices for returned products, prohibit advertising, require suppliers to give firm price quotes, prohibit proposals to clients of others or prohibit competitive bidding.

Standard-setting Programs are designed to "help customers obtain a means to measure value," and "to realize greater efficiency." They must be inclusive, with accessible standards, not exclusive; they should standardize to minimum levels; they need to be legal; and they require periodic review and monitoring. The operating structure of any standard-setting program needs to be governed by ethical and legal best practices, so the cost of participating has to be reasonable, not prohibitive; standards should have independent validation wherever possible; and participation in the program must be voluntary.

Standardization should only be used to judge performance, not the materials of production or the ways the product is used. The standards can't be used to fix prices, and must be updated regularly. You also need to permit participation in any standard-setting program by nonmembers and foreign competitors. Know how to structure this type of program in such a way as to keep it equitable, and to protect your association from liability risks.

From the recommended reading list, the book entitled *Membership Essentials: Recruitment, Retention, Roles, Responsibilities, and Resources* should be reviewed completely as part of your study sessions on this domain. The *Association Law Book* addresses standards development in chapter 60, while chapter 52-55, 58, 66, 71 and 72 cover membership issues plus antitrust compliance. The book *Professional Practices in Association Management* addresses membership in chapter 30, and globalization in chapter 31. *The Jossey-Bass Handbook* looks at internationalization in chapter 5, and ethics in chapter 9. In addition, I recommend that you review *How Are your Ethics?* and Mark Levin's *Millennium Members: How to Attract and keep Members in the New Marketplace* to do comprehensive study for questions in this domain.

CHAPTER 11

DOMAIN 8: PROGRAMS, PRODUCTS, AND SERVICES

Because there are so many types of programs, products, and services that may be offered by associations, and because the CAE accreditation certifies an executive's capacity to manage a wide variety of organizations, this domain is full of numerous parts and sub-sections. You should expect questions from this subject area to comprise 12-14% of the examination.

Before addressing the steps for developing services or programs, a CSE should always begin with a series of questions linked to **best practices**: is the product or program legal, ethical and still relevant; who does it serve; are the best practices unique to its area of production or presentation; and "what is the abandonment scenario?" You should know the value and specifics of doing a needs assessment or research, as mentioned earlier, in order to evaluate any program or product, whether it is something you are contemplating, something underway that needs modification, or something no longer working that should perhaps be discontinued.

In any **program development** from an event to fundraising to affinity relationships, you want to know how to follow a viable process: the CSE needs to determine the objectives, tactics, goals and strategies for the program, plus identify the need through research, then plan, implement, and evaluate. Developmental needs should be prioritized based on your strategic plan and the outcomes that you and the Board seek to realize. Research is still the basis for your making decisions, so prepare to do the needs assessment necessary in order to inform your program planning and implementation. Determine whether each initiative is directed at members, or is instead designed to have some impact on or connection to the association's industry.

Part and parcel with your implementation plans is the allocation of resources. Where programs will generate or be supported by association revenue, know the **unrelated business income (UBI)** tax liability ramifications of those sources. Implementation planning also involves the logistics, of course, that are efficient and cost-effective; it involves, as well, the development of a project-based marketing plan focused on the specific product or service, its price, place and means of promotion in order to deliver, where possible, non-dues revenues to the association. The evaluation phase should always be built into your program planning, along with the metrics to determine whether this is something to continue, improve, or to abandon. Know the elements of an **abandonment matrix assessment.**

Fundraising, sponsorships, and development programs use both qualitative and quantitative data along with an understanding of why donors give, in order to identify whether a given fundraising vehicle matches the needs of your organization. Remember: not-for-profit is a tax status as determined by the IRS code; it is not a business model. The CSE must know how to develop and implement multi-pronged development programs and understand all of the terms, levers, and limitations to association fundraising.

Don't be afraid: fundraising can be learned, and even be enjoyable. Certainly it is great for any executive, in success. Donors—whether individuals or institutions administered by individuals—give because of their care for specific issues or your stated mission. Giving money is an expression of values or ideals, and a person's goals for effectuating change or social good. Rarely, we must remember, are gifts given purely for the tax write-off, although donations to 501-c-3s are tax deductible, while those to a 501-c-6 are business expenses.

A fundraising plan begins with identifying your donors and how they will be reached. It generally assigns roles to various staff and governing volunteers as regards contacting and developing each donor; it also sets standards for success. Fundraisers use the **LAI Principles of Fundraising** which involved **linkage,** any access to a potential donor through peer relationship, bridge, or other contact; **ability**, which is an evaluation of each donor's capacity to give based on their financial standings and other commitments; and **interest,** which is the potential donor's connection to or compassion for your association's mission and the work that you do or have done.

Fundraising plans do a similar evaluation of **foundations:** these 501-c-3 entities fulfill educational or charitable needs that sometimes involve accepting corporate or government donations for distribution to other non-profit organizations. Foundations also have criteria for giving and requesting support; this is generally guided by their donor's intent. They are tapped by **grant writing,** which involves a professional proposal that persuades the foundation to give money by describing your program, the need for it, the implementation plan, the budget, and the percentage of its expense that you want from this institution. You should know how to establish a foundation, or 501-c-3, within other non-profit frameworks in the event you need one to receive corporate or government donations not otherwise available under your incorporation structure.

There are various types of fundraising programs that are germane to this subject area. An **annual fund** generates money for ongoing support; it involves attracting new donors, renewing past gifts, and inspiring supporters to increase their level of sponsorship from one year to the next. **Special events** like awards banquets of fundraising dinners may contribute to the annual fund; they connect your donors concretely to the association by showing something off or seeing leadership and supporters together which generates some social capital, as well. These annual gifts are generally unrestricted, so may be used for programs as well as for the administration to run them.

By contrast, a **capital campaign** is fundraising specifically for a building, whether to purchase or renovate one, or for significant equipment. It sets out to run for a specific period of time, although it can welcome multi-year pledges that accrete to a substantial amount in support of the capital effort.

Endowments are funds designed around a theme or issue where fundraising efforts go towards creating the endowed principle, which is invested in a way that permits the interest to support a program or endeavor. There are both restricted and unrestricted endowments. They may include **special gifts,** which are unique as the title suggests, and are often restricted to a specific purpose. **Planned giving** puts your association and its future fundraising needs into the documents of a will or estate, for donation at a later date, often after the death of its donor. Solicitation of these gifts are from current assets, but request that stock, property, or insurance benefits be made in the form of a contract or trust.

Planning meetings and holding events are major activities of associations and their CSEs, so you must know how to develop a program that aligns with an event's purpose, and how to tailor content to your audience that ensures that the event is the best way or in the best place to share whatever information is planned. You need to know how to supervise the logistics of any event successfully.

Your program, format, and speakers should grow out of the purpose of the convening and the audience it is meant to reach. So, whether a big conference or a strategic meeting, know the objectives of the gathering, the demographic or marketing profile of the intended audience, any history of this group convening (is it a reunion? An annual conference? A quarterly meeting?), determine the site where it will take place and the components of that site that will ensure success and appropriate access, then be sure to take a measure of whether there is any remote or cloud-based participation possible, either synchronously or asynchronously.

Site selection should be informed by the purpose of your meeting and its target audience; the general (technical, size, etc.) needs as well as any safety requirements and ADA accommodations; the economics of a given site including food and beverage, room rental rates for overnight stays, parking or travel issues, etc.; and any tax implications, including venues in foreign countries or on board cruises.

Know the strategies available to enhance your event's revenue, if that is its ambition, and to minimize attrition. This may include the pegging of registration fees, the sales of sponsorships, and rentals to exhibitors. Marketing may be supported by **list rental** of other groups in exchange for some cross promotion, or sponsors may be committed pending a rental of your list. Since any association's "primary knowledge component is its database," be sure that you understand the elements of a list rental policy, and whether you would share yours, in what format, and for how much.

Recognize the **disadvantages of endorsing vendor products and services,** as associations may grant third parties permission to use their names or logos as part of a sponsorship exchange. **Product endorsements** appear as though the association vouches for a product's efficacy or safety. Know the ways in which this may expose an association to product and tax liability issues. Evaluate whether the market power of your endorsement could be construed as anti-competitive; whether you have tort liability if your endorsement conveys some kind of expert authority that links you to future claims of negligence; and whether there are UBIT tax implications for revenues generated.

Know the elements of managing and operating an event, meeting, or banquet including the components of an event budget, F&B calculations, hotel expenses, and on-site logistics. The **Banquet Event Order (BEO)** is a document used by all hotels and other venues to specify all of the details of your event, room by room, hour by hour, day by day, meal by meal. It acts as a contract, and is created by the facility; be sure that you know how to read and evaluate them, even if you use a meeting planner. There can be hundreds of them for just a weekend conference (in multiple rooms on one site), but the details are invaluable for ensuring the smooth setup and accommodation of your guests.

Most major events and venue rentals are covered by **contracts** that need to comply with the ADA: ensure that your meeting or program participants have an opportunity to tell you what they need, so that you and the venue can make reasonable attempts to accommodate them. Contracts include an **offer,** an **acceptance,** and **consideration** or remuneration. Where you have large shipments to haul, exhibitions and trade shows also need a contract with a **drayage** firm. Check exhibit hall and hotel contracts for any financial consequences levied when things are shipped too early.

Of course, know the elements of a post-meeting or post-event evaluation. Be aware of the concept of an **open space meeting,** which sometimes takes place within the structure of a larger conference or convening. It is a self-organization strategy that permits a group to grapple with issues or ideas quickly. There is technology available for open space meetings; it can establish an agenda quickly, and help to create a plan of action going forward.

A **credentialing program** has to be ethical, fair, legal, and meet a need. The **need** for it arises out of the marketplace and your particular audience. It should be designed in order to "improve the quality of professional competence within the areas represented" by your association, and should ensure that an "individual exhibits mastery of a specific body of knowledge."

While that is the **purpose** of a credentialing program, its **objectives** should be to award recognition, establish credibility, raise the standards in your field, and potentially generate revenues back to the association. The components of its **criteria** should be "no more stringent than necessary to assume minimum qualifications," "must not restrict or boycott competitors," and should be established "only after reasonable notice and opportunity to participate is afforded to all potentially affected."

There are four main **types of credentialing programs**. The Certified Association Executive designation is a **certification;** it is accorded to people who meet an objective standard of competency through eligibility criteria, an examination, and meeting ethical guidelines. Certification may be accompanies by a designation or certificate, and is sometimes called **credentialing**. **Accreditation** is applied to "systems, organizations, and institutions," and refers to a "process of standards setting and compliance measurement.

Both accreditation and certification may expose an association to anti-trust liability, so make yourself aware of the legal ramifications in order to minimize risk. **Licensure** is a regulation program administered by some governmental agency. A **certificate** is distinct from certification; it usually involves attending or completing work on a training or professional development program; participants can be required to master certain aspects of the training.

There are guidelines for credentialing programs that militate against risk, and that also ensure that they meet technical standards that permit them to maintain reliability and validity. In order to establish a program, you need to identify the governing body, and then the job analysis or defined body of knowledge expected of each candidate. The administrative procedures need to be defined, along with any relevant policies, and the tenets for eligibility must be outlined clearly. How the evaluation will be measured must be set objectively to ensure that no candidate is "blackballed," or any competition limited.

Participation should be made voluntary in the program guidelines, and the credential open to nonmembers without prohibitive extra expense (that is, not enough difference to compel membership). Incorporating a code of conduct for candidates or affirmation to a code of ethics is recommended. Candidates should be selected through some process of application and evaluation, and should all be treated equally. Applications need to be decided upon by an objective body, and it should not be comprised only of credentialed people, or anyone who could gain financially from decisions that affect competitors.

If there are needs for renewal, maintenance, or ongoing skills development, they should be defined as part of the program definition, along with any provisions for revocation and reinstatement. Denials of credential should be made by written notice, and include the reasons, remedies, and process of appeal. Detail due process in the program design, including the opportunity for both sides to present evidence, and the right to cross-examine or carry on dialogue with those responsible for denying the credential. The scope of technical standards necessary or measured in advance of awarding the credential need to be spelled out in detail Associations should be careful not to promote those who *are* credentialed by name, or to single out in any negative way those that are not.

Make note of any legal implications of founding or maintaining a credentialing program. Issues that apply include fairness, confidentiality, ADA compliance, and anti-trust. Also be aware of conflicts of interest, both the perception of same as well as the reality. The *Association Law Handbook* covers certification in chapter 68, and accreditation of programs in chapter 69. Product certification is discussed in chapter 61.

Affinity Programs are an association's sponsorship of a commercial company's product or services. As mentioned earlier, these come with marketing benefits, but also potential liabilities. You will need to know how to establish policies and criteria for selecting affinity programs that are consistent with your association's "vision and mission."

Selection starts with identifying a need, and then the appropriate fit of product to stakeholder community. Where there are unique advantages for members of the product or service, this may be advantageous to an association's marketing strategy;

however, where the association is involved directly or actively in marketing a product, tax liabilities may accrue. When evaluating an affinity program, it is important to define just what the marketing commitment will be for the association, and then how to evaluate the program's success on both sides. Estimating the revenue back to the association is an important factor in selecting an affinity program.

Because this is a revenue-generating proposition in some manner and fashion, the CSE is responsible for understanding the UBIT liabilities. Sometimes there are royalties; in other instances there may be active marketing that is taxed. Review the *Association Law Handbook* chapter 77 on affinity programs.

Finally, **Professional Development Programs and Delivery Systems** will be tested in this domain. You will be expected to know how to develop and improve the content of professional development products from seminars to curricula and publications that meet the needs of your constituency and the requirements of your industry or field. This includes preventive education that helps members maintain compliance with various applicable laws and regulations, as in **in-service training** for your membership.

There are numerous ways to conduct these programs that are called their **delivery systems.** These included face-to-face workshops, distance learning, self-directed learning, and web-based courses. Of course, know the terms for all of the current multi-platform learning technologies including virtual instruction, podcasts, webcasts or live event feeds, webinars, and blogs. These are pretty common in the cultural currency now, but be aware of any new developments and tools.

Distance education includes online courses, but also videoconferences, teleconferences, and written correspondence courses—anything where student and teacher are technically separated either by space, time, or both. **Blended learning** is some combination of non-synchronous and face-to-face instruction.

You should know that adults learn differently from children. **Pedagogy** is the approach conventionally taken to teach kids, where the teacher is dominant, and the student does not change or interact with the curriculum development, per se.

Andragogy is more relevant to an association's programs, because it approaches the student as an adult and gets them involved in the design of their program. Adults only remember a percentage of the information conveyed to any given sense, so successful professional development programs "tell, show, do, then review." You will ensure near 90% retention on information that adult students see, hear, say for themselves, and then do in some way.

Because adults are purpose-driven, self-directed, ready and motivated to learn, they need educational programs that are both life-centered (and relevant to their work life) and experience-centered, for maximum retention and application. In order to feel safe, adults need physical and psychological comfort in an environment where they feel supported and respected. In order to stay engaged, they need active involvement and feedback, as one gets in breakout groups outside of a lecture or teacher-to-group presentation.

Structured group discussions and collaborations with peers have been shown to be optimal in teaching adults. Pre-test self-assessments are also useful because they can activate an adult student's "need to know." Above all, they want practical applications for material presented. You will be expected to be able to incorporate your understanding of the conditions necessary for successful adult learning into creating professional development content.

An important strategy for the design process of instructional systems is called "**ADDIE:** Analysis (e.g., is there a market for this program), Design, Development, Implementation, Evaluation." Like SPIE, it is somewhat self-evident and circular, but lays out your steps in a simple mnemonic. **Evaluation** has four components in varying degrees that can look like a pyramid. The first, largest level is **reaction,** followed by **learning,** then **behavior,** and the top, smallest level being **results.**

The core tasks for the CSE as regards professional development, then, are to evaluate and plan multiple methods of program delivery and content; to develop and enhance your association's offerings; to create positive conditions for adult learning; and to implement preventive education (like sexual harassment sensitivity training).

One book on the recommended reading list addresses professional development programs directly: *Core Competencies in Association Professional Development,* by Terri Tracey, CAE, and Kathleen M. Edwards, CAE. In addition, chapter 26 in *Professional Practices in Association Management* also covers education programs. In the Cox, also review chapter 15 on fundraising, chapter 16 on supplier relations, chapter 32 on meeting planning, and chapters 33-35 on certification and accreditation. Program evaluations are discussed in *The Jossey-Bass Handbook,* chapter 16; fundraising in chapters 17-18.

CHAPTER 12

DOMAIN 9: MARKETING, PUBLIC RELATIONS, AND COMMUNICATIONS

This final testing domain umbrellas a number of topics. While marketing was touched upon in the subject content of domain 1 around concepts of branding, (and while it was formerly tested in domain 1 of earlier CAE exams), it is now part of domain 9, the subject area dedicated to **public relations,** which are programs that are designed for the public at large, and **communications,** which include publications and the media generally directed at members and stakeholders. 8-10% of the CAE examination will be devoted to questions from this domain.

Discussions of **marketing** often begin with the "Four Ps:" the **product** that you are offering; the **price**, which is determined by your product's true cost in order to ensure that your association receives a modest return; the **place** where you distribute this product; and the **promotion,** which, more and more, must be targeted to the audience or consumer for your product. The start of your marketing process is to **define the market scope,** the first step of which being to do an **environmental scan.** The scan involves identifying the **standards** of excellence expected by your members or consumers; then the **fitness** to need, such as which services are needed and concomitantly valued by your stakeholders as a means to excellence; and, analyzing **trends** or future needs so as to be ahead of the curve in your market segment.

To the environmental scan, you must add the internal and external influences being brought to bear on your product and its market. Your **internal**

data involves the structure of your association's workflow through staff and volunteers; your corporate **culture;** and the **resources** that you have available, your potential capital outlay to bring a product to market.

The **external influences** include the **econosphere** or world market; the **sociosphere;** the **technosphere** and how that may impact distribution or automated production; the **politosphere;** and the **biosphere** or physical environment. The final component of defining your market scope involves **setting limitations,** as a consequence of your scan, data, and influences; these may involve limiting your definition of the market share, your outreach, or other parameters.

The next step towards building a marketing plan, once you know the scope of your product, is to recognize and articulate the **value proposition** that is promised by your association. These are not the features of the organization: **features** list all of the attributes of a product or event, like all of the speakers or workshops available at your annual conference. **Benefits** "define the positive results that may come from those features"; while **value** focuses on "the specific impact that the product or service will deliver" to individual members or customers."

How do you assess the ROI for members of your association and its products? One strategy is the membership survey, which can be very focused on what you do or might do for the field, but it must be done on a regular basis. Focus groups can be enlisted, and **retention calls** placed to current, prospective or lapsed members to do phone surveys or interviews. If you already have a product, benefit, or service in the field, you can **track its usage.** Finally, new products can be **tested** in small markets in order to learn about their viability and public reception.

While the branding and positioning covered in the first domain related to the association as a whole, for this section you need to understand the concepts as they relate both to an institution as well as to a product, service, or publication. **Branding** is the promise of consistency to an audience; some would say, a sacred promise.

The great thing about a brand is that it saves the time of staff and stakeholders because it communicates what your audience can expect, clearly and honestly. On the other hand, to maintain a great brand requires focused management because branding happens whether it is supervised or not, so you want to control that process to your advantage.

A **marketing plan** is discussed at length in chapter 29 of *Professional Practices in Association Management*. Put simply, it is an action plan for reaching your target group. It has an introduction, a summary of your business, the research accumulated above regarding the product and audience, then marketing strategies and projections, and monitoring or evaluation techniques.

There are a number of types of marketing that you should understand for this test. **One-to-One marketing** is a lot like it sounds, as it is customer-focused, but has four critical components. When selling to customers, this strategy looks at the needs your product can satisfy, then uses what information you have accumulated about your customer and their trust in you to "increase 'share of wallet,'" by making additional sales.

This strategy invests actual cash in customer retention, because it is a small amount compared to customer acquisition, in order to "increase the durability of customer relationships." This strategy is not retail focused: it is customer focused, so it involves adding to the things you have to offer in response to the market, and "increases your product offerings to the customer." Finally, it creates "an interactive relationship that leads to meeting more customer needs," a cyclical pattern that rewards customers for their telling you more about themselves that will lead to your offering them more of the products that they want.

Permission marketing also involves a customer relationship, where in the consumer is offered the chance for you to market to them, and encouraged to participate in interactive marketing campaigns through rewards like discounts and coupons. Permission marketing starts at your first customer contact, and seeks to expand the permissions granted to the marketer by the customer, with success being measured by the depths of permissions rather than number of sales.

Target marketing involves the selection of an audience segment, then developing a strategy and position specific to each segment. This strategy often arises out of **segmentation research** which involves "identifying bases for segmenting; developing profiles of those segments; then developing measures of segment attractiveness."

Some associations benefit from **cause-related marketing,** wherein companies exercise their corporate social responsibility through alliances with social change non-profit organizations. The benefits to an association are the marketing budgets and spotlights directed at their programs or issue.

For the exam, be sure that you know how to define the scope of your association market and any target segments or stakeholder groups to which you would direct your marketing strategies. Know how to apply research and other environmental or marketplace scanning tools in the evolution of your marketing plan, and know the ways in which that plan can support your association's branding and position, as it relates to recruiting and retaining members, and developing or promoting programs.

Your association's **strategic public relations program** should embrace the "art of reputation management," and the "planned effort to influence public opinion through good character and responsible performance," in the form of a two-way communication. To develop your public relations program, be expected to identify the key publics that need to be reached, and know that the strongest strategies limit that list to three.

Each public identified will require **message framing** that is unique: "key and secondary messages to motivate the target audience in taking actions that your organization desires." Since PR is the "management of communication between an organization and its publics," it is often referred to as **communications.** It is coming to leverage and becoming involved with **social media,** which is evolving from being members talking to other members into a strategic communications platform for associations, as well.

Public relations involves **publicity,** which is the free dissemination of information through news and social media, and is traditionally the least controlled portion of your PR. **Advertising** is paid communications, completely controlled, but only a one-way interaction. **Marketing,** as I discussed earlier, is also a one-way communication process with the ambition of inspiring consumers to purchase specific products or services, or even ideas and positions.

Promotion is a blend of PR and marketing that umbrellas special events and activities that build a market's interest in a certain organization or product or cause. As I covered in chapter 9, **government relations** involves communications with any of the branches of government, **lobbying** is those communications with the intent to influence regulations or legislation, while **public affairs** is the government term for public relations.

PR is relational: it has various publics, as I mentioned, and terms that refer to communications with each broad constituency. Know that **community relations** are your communications with individuals and groups "within your association's area of operation;" **media relations** obviously involves the press; and **industry relations** are those with other organizations in your field or sector.

To develop a PR program, you need to identify which are the individuals or groups that you want to influence. The SPIE strategy is effective here again in order to do a first internal and external scan and any research that can contribute to your answering that question. As you establish objectives for your PR program, be sure that these goals coincide with those of your mission and organization. These may involve influencing stakeholders, enhancing the public trust, changing opinion around an issue or situation, increasing awareness of your organization or industry, and calling for action or reaction. Awareness, Understanding, Attitudes and Behavior are the top four goals, with the last being the most difficult to change.

Next, you need to identify your key audience, and focus your plan on those segments or publics you seek to reach, always seeking to enhance your public trust. You cannot communicate with everyone, so identify the audiences most vital to your association and its ambitions. It is advised to involve your leadership and key volunteers in the selection of these publics and, together, to establish and manage the reach of your messaging in a realistic way.

You will find, upon doing this sort of scan, that you will have lots of targets to choose from, starting with your members and customers, to government and association leaders, then the government and the public at large. Know that you will need to design specific communications strategies for each of those audiences, and also establish measurable SMART goals for each audience. Determine *how* you are going to say *what,* and to *whom.* For every one of your objectives, develop a message strategy and a media strategy.

PR planning then involves designing your process of implementation: assigning responsibilities both as regards internal procedures and staffing, and as regards external relations; designing a delivery timeline; developing any relevant budgets; and then doing a test scenario before your official launches. Once complete, you need to have an evaluation strategy that measures both the process and your progress so that you can incorporate the results of your PR plan for incorporation into your future endeavors and communications.

There are a variety of **communications channels:** media relations, for example, is one of the **external channels,** and involves providing the press with information and with experts that are, collectively, reliable, interesting, prompt, and useful. The tools available for media relations include the **press release,** a document written in inverted pyramid style that details the who, what, where, when, and how of an event or situation; a **media advisory,** which is a simpler document that identifies the 5 W's in bullet form; a **press**

conference, which is an assembly of reporters for a particularly newsworthy announcement or revelation; and **individual relationships with the media.**

When giving media interviews, a CSE should designate a spokesperson who has been media trained; deliver three or less clear message points; stay on message; <u>never</u> count on something being or staying "off the record"; do not say "no comment," but do remain silent or say "I don't know," when necessary," dress well for on camera purposes, and stay positive.

The other external channel of communication is **crisis management;** the CAE exam requires that you know how to develop a **crisis communications and management plan** in order to communicate the position of your association as regards the situation. Once you identify your association's upfront risks, the objective of your crisis management is to "present and maintain a positive image of the organization; deliver timely, accurate and current information; monitor all channels of communication and address inaccuracies; and maintain the support of key stakeholders."

Of paramount importance is that the CSE know how to stay in control during a crisis. It is recommended that you know how to "proactively contact the media and accept all media inquiries; establish a media command center; get the facts before making statements; neither lie, speculate, or stonewall; be cautious about drawing conclusions; and admit when you don't have the information but commit to finding out."

Your websites, digital assets strategy, and integrated publications program, by contrast, are the internal communication channels that you and your association are responsible for. As regards an **integrated publications program,** you must know how to evaluate consumer and trade media outlets, and develop and implement media approaches that advance the goals of your organization.

First, determine your editorial mission: are you just disseminating news and information? Providing practical information that your professionals can use in their work lives? Advocating on issues and sharing your organization's position? Or using the media instruments to promote your association's services or programs? Second, you need to identify the key audiences that any publication (on any platform, at this point) will address. Some have a targeted and controlled circulation. Others address a segment of your stakeholders organized around specific skills or interests. Many association publications are for the general members.

Next, consider what type of periodicals you could or should generate. Some associations still do print newsletters or magazines, either with or without external advertising for revenue generation and cost management. More prevalent now are eNewsletters or eZines. Tabloid newspapers, bulletins or e-Alerts are also options, whether periodically or regularly. Academic and scientific associations may sponsor a peer-reviewed journal.

Other formats are coming online in light of digital delivery methods, like blogs, podcasts, videos, etc. Before you expand your selection of platforms for your integrated publications program, also review those periodicals already generated by your organization.

Next, consider the financial goals of your publications program. Do you need to make a profit? Can you break even, or is there an amount that equals an acceptable loss? If you are using this to be a profit center, what level of revenue do you accept, and will you accept advertising in order to reach those goals? You must be aware of UBIT implications, so it is always advised to consult an attorney as part of your evaluation of this element of a publication plan. You will need to separate editorial income from advertising income, because net advertising income is generally subject to UBIT. Finally, you need to assess whether selling subscriptions outside of your membership will impact or dilute the audience for your publication, or in what way impact membership recruitment?

It is important that you understand some terms that are related to communications law, and that you review chapter 33 in the *Association Law Book* that covers publications and copyrights. **Copyright** is the "legal protection afforded an original work set in some tangible form." **Invasion of privacy** is "publishing the names or photos of individuals in association publications that may invade their rights of privacy." Your protection against that is requiring signed release forms from anyone discussed or photographed, and to have **liability insurance,** which protects your association "against claims related to publishing activities."

The truth is your best defense: **libel** is a published statement that "declares persons to be dishonest, fraudulent, or immoral;" **slander** is "an oral statement that defames, misrepresents, or otherwise vilifies another person." But we live in a litigious society, so releases, insurance, and other protections are the CSE's responsibility.

When a staff member produces an article for your newsletter, this material is considered the property of the employer and is called **work for hire.** There is a recently expanded exception to copyright law called **fair use,** wherein copyrighted material may be used on a limited basis, such as educational purposes, or as excerpts in reviews. It is important to be aware that **information of competitive value** must be made available to non-members, in order to avoid exposure to restraint of trade or anti-trust liability, although you are not obligated to promote it to them, and you are permitted to charge them higher fees for access.

Your **website development strategy** also falls under the heading of an internal communication structure, and needs some fundamental thinking by the CSE in order to develop a plan for its creation and management. For many associations, this is one of the most effective and feasible communication formats for accomplishing your goals and meeting member needs, in association with some member-directed messaging. You do need to establish the mission or purpose of your website, and how that connects to the overall mission of the organization. You need to know the key audiences for that site, whether members or the broader public that may use it to gather information about the association and its issues of concern. Once you know your audiences, you should establish their needs, and how your website can meet those needs. Finally, once you have a website designed and launched, you need to determine how it will be regularly updated and by whom i.e. who will "own" it.

For the CAE exam, you will be expected to know the basic terminology that pertains to web activity and management. **New media** describes the various communications done electronically and digitally through new technologies and devices like **wikis,** which are websites that are communally edited, and **RSS feeds,** a technical standard that stands for "really simple syndication," and distributes website headlines as XML documents.

Media by itself, or **"traditional media"** refers to print, broadcast, and film. The **internet** is of course, the worldwide web, a digital network between computers and other electronic platforms that send and receive messages and other information. An

intranet is an internal network that provides similar electronic or digital communications, to a specific and limited set of users. A **portal** is a website "used as an entry point to other websites, often as a search engine." A **newsreader** is a program that permits you to read multiple RSS feeds and updates, so that dozens of sites can be followed in a single screen. A **blog** is an online "journal...of short text entries added by a single author." Some include comment vehicles that make it a two-way form of communication. **Spam** is unsolicited or junk email. Some limit the definition to "junk newsgroup postings," but that's not common parlance; only federal legislation has jurisdiction presently over spamming.

Additional reading that I think you will find helpful in reviewing the content of this domain includes chapters 22, 27 and 28 of *Professional Practices in Association Management,* and chapter 33 in the *Association Law Handbook,* plus *Nonprofit Marketing Best Practices* by John Burnett. UBIT rules, copyright law, libel and slander, and member

v. non-member issues should be understood, from a legal point of view, when preparing for the test. Chapter 12 of *The Jossey-Bass Handbook* covers marketing, as well.

CHAPTER 13

DIVERSITY & INCLUSION: THE BIG SIX STRATEGIES FOR SUCCESS

For Associations and organizations, diversity and inclusion (D&I) have become a key business strategy because of its intrinsic link both to an institution's growth and success but also due to the ways in which D&I creates value for stakeholders, members, and other constituents of a company's efforts. The demographics of the United States are increasingly multi-cultural which means, in part, that associations and their executives can develop new products and a broader scope of services for an ever-growing, expanding, and differentiating marketplace. In order to access these opportunities, however, a CAE needs to understand how to develop a strategy for knowing and connecting to these communities, and how to implement a D&I approach within their institutions, as well.

THE NEW NORMAL

Given the changing demographics in today's markets and workforce, Diversity and Inclusion (D&I) must be top-of-mind at any thriving Association that seeks to remain competitive and relevant. The United States has always been a melting pot of cultures and ethnicities. But white male Anglo-Saxons continue to thrive as the majority culture in most US-based Associations. Oftentimes, when you're the majority culture, you define yourself, your world views, and your priorities as "**normal**." But then, this problem arises: ***where does that leave everyone else***?

The US demographic reality is this: by 2016, the "majority culture" will no longer look like it once did.

70% percent of the workforce will be women and/or African American and Latino.[1] In addition, your "marketplace" and membership pool is now defined by the fact that, for the first time in American history, less than half of all newborns are non-Hispanic Caucasian. The percentage of our citizens who are white (non-Hispanic) is shrinking, year to year, particularly among the young. By 2050, people of color will constitute the majority of our population.[2]

What happens to "normal" then?

This demographic shift already impacts our politics and economy daily. Not only are diverse minority groups increasing as a percentage of the US population, but the economic power that they wield is expanding, as well. So, anyone who fails to fully embrace the "New Normal" of these changing demographics will also fail to capitalize on the substantial growth in buying power, association membership, workforce talent, philanthropy and gifts that these diverse markets represent.

The 2010 Census determined that 36% of our population was already "minority": 16% Latino, 12%

African American, and 5% Asian American; 2% identify as members of two or more ethnic or racial minorities, and 1% as other ethnicities. In addition, over 8 million white immigrants reside in the US; they represent additional diverse perspectives as well as, in many cases, key Association constituencies. Currently, African-Americans are the largest minority among adults over age 50; this represents "a major turning point for American society."[3] In the under-50 crowd, Latinos comprise the largest group, after non-white Europeans.

It is also important to understand that the US's burgeoning diversity is no longer about immigration. The white population component is aging and having fewer children as compared with parents of any other ethnic or racial group. States like California, New Mexico, Hawaii and Texas are already majority minority (60%, 55%, 77% and 60%, respectively). Many others are on the verge, including New Jersey, Nevada, Arizona, Georgia, and Maryland. Cities like the New York metropolitan area are 51% minority, the Los Angeles area is 68%, Houston 60%, and

Miami-Ft. Lauderdale 65%. And fully 28 of the 50 most populous US counties are majority minority including the top three, led by Los Angeles County at 72%.[4]

We call this demographic and cultural reality the **New Normal.** The upshot of it is that any CAE and his/her Association will encounter very real problems and disadvantages unless they have a comprehensive ***strategy for diversity and inclusion***. Any Association that thinks that the Old Normal is the Still Normal is destined to find its capacity to deliver on its mission gravely impacted. These organizations will be eclipsed by competitors that have embraced the New Normal and incorporated D&I into key aspects of their business, from staffing and customer relations to marketing and supplier alliances.

A good understanding of the New Normal is essential because it is the ***first step towards rooting out subtle bias and bigotry.*** We can no longer use the former Caucasian mainstream as our benchmark for quality, competence, or "club membership." We can't evaluate non-white executive candidates by feigning surprise that they're "so articulate." We can't use HR phrases like "more than just the normal applicants." We need to identify where vestiges of the Old Normal remain in our management thinking, Association policies, and stakeholder interactions.

I believe that it is essential that today's CSE master the ways in which D&I can help every initiative in their organization. It is a business decision: D&I enhances your brand and supports your institutional and financial targets, inside and out, along with **retention** of the very best staffers, members and skills, **productivity** and **innovation**. This chapter will cover some of the ways it does so. Personally, I had great success organizing a D&I framework for my Association, and since then have assembled the following set of strategies and best practices which I believe can also help your organization become and remain successful and competitive in your market segment.

You can find all of this information including more metrics and deeper explanations in my book

Diversity & Inclusion: The Big Six Strategies for Success. But let me share some of the critical highlights that will support your study on the CAE exam.

Fundamentally, **diversity** is the way in which an organization mixes and appreciates the wide variety of assets that redound to it by the similarities and differences between all people with whom we engage. There is no fixed definition. Some people explain it as "a wide range of interests, backgrounds, experiences." Others describe it as "differences among groups of people and individuals based on ethnicity, race, socioeconomic status, gender, exceptionalities, language, religion, sexual orientation, and geographical area." The term definitely embraces the variety of human and institutional viewpoints, backgrounds, and life experiences, as well as a "tolerance of thought, ideas, people with differing viewpoints, backgrounds, and life experiences." Diversity also includes differences of opinions, backgrounds, religious and political beliefs, sexual orientation, heritage, and life experience.

Diversity concerns are certainly not unique to associations: all organizations, whether for-profit or non-profit, encounter and incorporate diversity. **Inclusion** is the second part of this strategic priority. It is the idea of creating a supportive, welcoming environment within any institution in order to encourage the highest level of contribution and participation towards your organization's services and mission. Many Associations are finding that D&I is so much a part of their vision for service and success that they now go so far as to embrace it as one of their *core values.*

D&I require a CSE's structured institutional plan and deep attention in part because the upside is so substantial: your organization will be healthier and more successful, internally, plus be able to access and serve a much broader, more holistic marketplace. Some of the focused attention to D&I is necessary, however, because this is a challenging part of an executive's management responsibility. Some aspects of diversity are readily apparent like age, race, and gender. Some attributes like skills or thinking/learning style are discernible through interviews or experience with a colleague or employee. But the vast majority of diverse attributes—I'd say, nearly 90%—are "invisible." Your employees' family relationships and values, your customers' personality and sexual orientation, your colleagues' job history and communication style are all hidden upon first meeting. But your responsibility, in organizing a D&I strategy, is to lead your association in critical strategies to incorporate the backgrounds and working styles of those with various experiences and socio-cultural make-up.

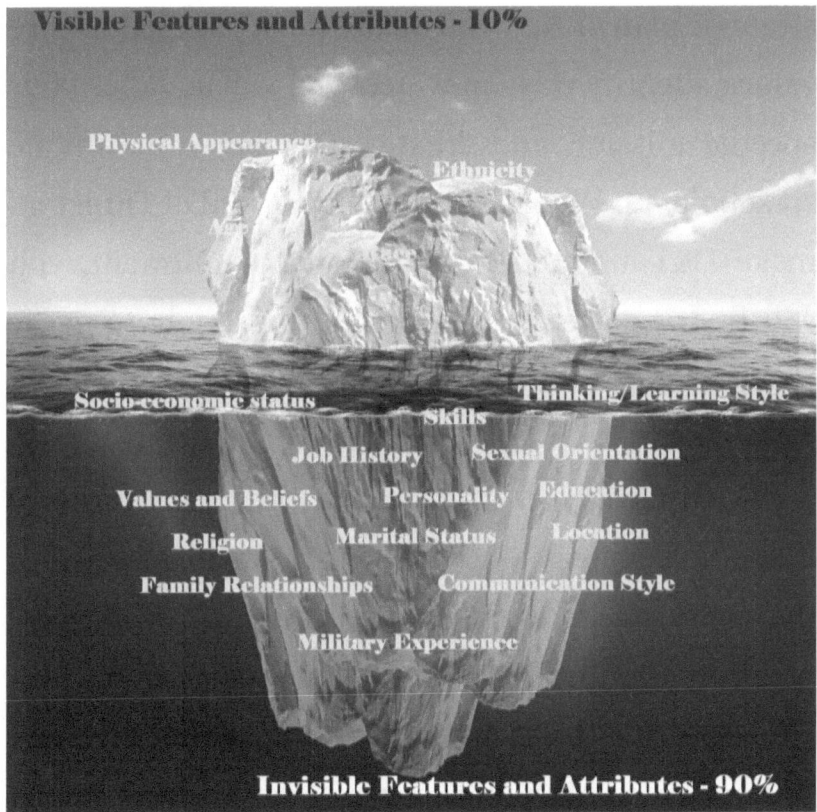

The bottom line here is that attention to D&I is the right thing to do, *and* it's invariably the right thing for your Association, as well.

The first thing that will assist you in your efforts at leveraging D&I successfully within your organization is to *make it a key business strategy*. Just like other key objectives that you outline in your strategic plan or that you delineate in your list of core values, identify ways in which D&I will advance your specific mission and create value for your unique stakeholders. When you and your Board of Directors make D&I a stated institutional commitment, you will find it easier to implement and apply to every financial, HR, and programmatic decision that you make.

A **diversity statement** is an organization's individual expression of what diversity means within the rubric of their mission, and it makes concrete precisely what will flow from your Association's D&I efforts. It is a **best practice** to post this diversity statement in all public forums and social media platforms where your organization and its mission are found. This includes your employee handbook and your website, as well as in any materials that your Association generates for programs or volunteers.

If you are leading a strategic development effort for your organization's D&I, it is interesting to do research on the many ways that associations construct their diversity statement. I include a wide variety of examples in my book, and encourage you to use it as a resource, if you are starting this undertaking without one yet in place.

The very same thought process applies to developing your institution's policies around inclusion, too. In particular, you want to look at all the aspects of your Association's environment in order to identify the ways in which it can include and encourage a wide range of perspectives and participation. Elucidate the ways in which this sort of commitment to inclusion ties directly to your organization's mission, and how it supports and enhances the social purpose and objectives that you have set out to accomplish.

Beyond just laying out a definition, it is important to define for yourselves how it is that an effective D&I strategy can play an essential role in achieving whatever you consider your business purposes. You can begin by making an assessment of your particular organization's strategic direction or business initiatives, and then explore the ways in which your D&I strategy can play a role in their success. As part of this review, you will fulfill every Association's imperative to foster an inclusive, respectful workplace that inspires creativity, productivity, and engagement. And you will build a set of solutions and tools for D&I that contribute to the future success of your organization on every level.

Part of your strategy development process involves identifying your **target audience for diversity.** This is done by analyzing every sector of your stakeholders: your audience, your service area, your employees and volunteer workers, and the markets where you can be found. You want to identify the "primary focus areas" for D&I within your own Association's operations and services. These may be along ethnic or racial lines, ability, or sexual orientation. There are so many dimensions to diversity, and your objective, as CSE leading the development of a D&I strategy, is to focus in on the ways that your policy and protocols will support and embrace the contributions that *any* stakeholder—staff and volunteers, suppliers and market—brings to your organization's mission and initiatives. Think broadly and include the broadest spectrum possible.

The following is a framework with **six components** that your Association can use to develop and expand the use of D&I to improve your business impact and further your mission. It is a comprehensive strategic approach, and one that is easy to adopt; it will embed Diversity and Inclusion into your specific workforce, workplace, suppliers, partners, and marketplace. This systematic plan also shows how to contribute to a positive Statement of Financial Activities and other key objectives of your organization through D&I.

The Big Six Strategy for Success is a framework that can help an Association and you, as CSE, to help you build and implement your D&I "plan of attack," one that helps align everyone involved in your work with this strategy, and one that can really improve your organization's success. Maybe *you* will be the CAE responsible for your institution's diversity, or maybe you will have a staff member or department dedicated to D&I. Either way, thinking through these

Big Six ideas will help you discover ways to inform, engage, and motivate everyone from staff to Board to volunteers in a clear way that both works well and delivers on more mission-related results. This strategy has been widely proven and is readily adaptable. Of course, I go into it and its applications in greater detail in *Diversity & Inclusion: The Big Six Strategy for Success*, but this gives you a great introduction for ways to embed diversity and inclusion into your specific environment!

STRATEGY 1: TALENT OPTIMIZATION

Your first commitment should be to inviting and embracing many diverse voices in all aspects of your association. Over-indexing in diversity on one front doesn't minimize the need to be inclusive in the others, nor does just a "sprinkling" of diverse volunteers or staff members bring the full force and benefit of D&I to your organization. I go into some of this in more detail in additional strategies below, but I encourage you to think not just HR and volunteer recruitment, but also about how diversity applies to your programs and services, to your publicity and marketing outreach, to the products you generate. You are an Association located in a big, diverse, and rapidly changing America. I encourage you to meditate on and embrace that in all its aspects.

So this first strategy, **Talent optimization** involves making a commitment to diverse talent on all relevant levels. This includes multi-cultural representation on committees, in departments, on your Board, and for top level executives as much as general staff and volunteers.

To realize this first strategy, a CSE needs to help set goals for diverse talent across every level and point that the Association touches. This is an essential step before you can outline how you will collectively meet those goals. Maybe you have a different D&I goal in a number of different areas. Or maybe there is an annualized goal for the Association, over all. Oftentimes a CSE or Board will develop bonus or financial incentives that are linked with various diversity targets. In other instances, line-items or full budgets are set aside to meet or support these goals.

STRATEGY #2: IMAGE

Your Association has an image that operates both internally to the organization and externally. It's a mind picture that anyone conjures in conjunction with your organization's name, and it contributes directly to how you "sell" your services or products. Public image is rarely fixed: it changes based on what it is that your Association does, how those activities are covered in the media, and what generally is said about your work and position in the non-profit landscape.

There are a lot of representations of your image. For example:

- Advertisements
- Physical images online or in media
- Optics at a public presentation or convention

- Graphics tied to your Association, or your specific logo
- The way that you are perceived by staff, volunteers or stakeholders

Even though your image is fluid, the second aspect of your D&I strategy is to recognize that you can analyze your **Association image**, and then direct, influence or change it. You want anything that the public sees—from programs to reports to ads to photos at your events to marketing releases—to reflect your commitment to D&I. Look around you. What photographs do you share on your website? Who is in your product brochures? What does your logo or conference key art say about the relationship between your organization and the diverse marketplace it serves?

Each department within your organization needs a set of goals around D&I for their own part in generating and maintaining your Association image. These need to stay at the forefront of all decision making in order to improve your image within the diverse communities with which you engage.

Remember to think through what translations might be appropriate to meet your D&I service goals. Look at ways to express not only racial diversity and ethnic representation but also your Association's inclusion of LGBT (lesbian, gay, bisexual and transgender) relationships and differences in ability.

Use your image strategy to share your Association's D&I success. Do special recognitions of diverse members of your Board or volunteers. Share your diversity statistics. Consider special events for diverse components of your community or stakeholders. This all contributes to enhancing your overall image through implementation of D&I.

STRATEGY #3: SUPPLIER DIVERSITY

CSE's and their Associations can leverage their economic capacity to support and enhance their D&I strategy. By setting goals to have diversity in the places we spend money and amongst the suppliers of services that we hire, CSE's can make diversification of their suppliers an important component of their overall D&I strategy. This goes beyond supporting your internal goals: it also enhances your visibility in diverse communities and improves your attractiveness to diverse audiences. These are going to have positive financial ramifications! Opening up new communities and opportunities will expand your own sales and services marketplace.

I ask that you look at who provides you with your Association goods, services, materials and awards because it is easy to keep on doing the same thing and dealing with the same people over time. In fact, many Associations say that they don't use women-owned suppliers or minority-owned businesses because they have long-standing relationships with non-diverse or male-owned companies and continue to find them familiar and reliable. This is not a criticism of your historical relationships or vendors. But in order to improve **supplier diversity**, you may need to branch out your purchases or RFPs.

I strongly believe that it is worth your effort to do so. One of the great correlates of supplier diversity is the way it introduces your Association and its services into entirely new markets, regions, or communities. You can also learn about new opportunities or regions through these suppliers, gaining access to more buying power or service opportunities. Supplier diversity contributes new resources to your organization.

STRATEGY #4: REGIONAL/COMMUNITY ENGAGEMENT

A natural outgrowth of your D&I strategy should be to explore all possible opportunities for your Association to meet, serve, and market to the diverse communities within your field of impact.

As you evaluate the various demographic sectors that can benefit from your services or that align with your mission, you may develop new programs or unique strategies to meet the needs and differences that you identify within your service sector or region.

As you bring your D&I initiatives to the regional or local level, you are bound to expand your Association's influence and success.

Begin by identifying the target communities for your D&I initiatives on a regional, state, and community level. Can you meet a need with your programs or services? Can doing so introduce your Association into new communities and markets? Or open up new opportunities?

This sort of engagement also applies to an Association's philanthropy. However you approach strategic giving, I encourage you to look at it through your D&I strategy lens. There may be ways to award scholarships or internships or other gifts tie to or that greatly enhance your overall engagement with a specific region or a variety of communities.

STRATEGY #5: STRATEGIC PARTNERSHIPS

Both corporations and Associations oftentimes make programmatic or financial partnerships with diverse organizations and communities. They do this in order to expand on the D&I aspect of their image, and in order to increase their customer or client base, including online in new social-media. It's been shown that making these partnerships also improves diverse hiring, inclusion and retention: it makes employees and volunteers feel valued when alliances or contributions are made in their communities; these partnerships also open up access to and information about diverse groups that can provide valuable talent introductions and marketing insights back to your Association.

This component of the Big Six Strategy teaches that **strategic partnerships** can bring to your Association a unique set of tools that will build diversity amongst your staff, your volunteers, your suppliers, your customers or served constituents, and your markets of operation and influence. I have found that Associations and their CSEs can partner with a wide variety of special-interest organizations as a way to build new relationships and enhance their efforts at recruitment in various sectors and demographics.

Many of us are aware of the benefits of receiving sponsorships and financial support from for-profit corporations. These can enhance your image, too, and raise your profile in communities and on platforms that your own marketing or publicity cannot reach, on its own. Remember that you are helping your partner/donor, too, so I encourage you to develop **best practices for sponsorships and partnerships** so you are aware of the mutual benefits and responsibilities of both parties.

The key to this strategic component is the **alignment of goals and values** between your Association and any partnering for-profit or other organization. You need to have a clear and detailed conversation about the tangible, expected benefits of all parties to any sponsorship or partnership. This should then be written down so that both sides can agree on what they will do or deliver, and what they expect as far as materials, reports, money, profit-sharing, publicity, etc. You may agree to co-brand marketing or other materials, but each side needs to ensure the consistency of their logo and other image-oriented collaterals.

Next, coordinate these partnerships with your stakeholders: your staff, board, committees and volunteers, plus your communities and service markets so that you ensure support and success for the initiative. And lastly, discuss what will be measured in this partnership, how, when, and by which party. I discuss some ideas both below and in my book about D&I measurements; other metric strategies have been reviewed here in earlier chapters. The point of this reminder is that, in a successful partnership, everyone wants to know how well it worked and when that progress will be evaluated. So discuss it up front for optimal strategic benefit.

STRATEGY #6: TRAINING & DEVELOPMENT

D&I is often a component of staff training. A successful D&I strategy includes education amongst all stakeholders so that they are active participants in realizing all of the Association's D&I goals and objectives. That is the key to ensuring success.

Many organizations do orientations or trainings on a variety of core values and practices. Diversity has the same requirement. CSEs need to look out over their entire organization and identify the points at which training or information sessions will propel their diversity goals. It's not just the job of HR! D&I is successful—and will *bring* success to your mission and bottom line—when it is a pervasive part of your corporate culture. This will ensure that your organization attracts and keeps the most skilled, passionate, and dedicated people.

Even today, part of D&I training involves raising awareness about and fostering positive relationships between diverse people. Not everyone knows everything about those who are unlike themselves in some way. But you want them to work together constructively and productively, and that begins with understanding, appreciation, and positive relationships amongst everyone in your Association.

And you need to know how your organization is doing, from the inside. Many institutions use regular assessment tools or do a **cultural audit** in order to give managers the data to understand and improve their inclusion and retention.

I have an extensive chapter in *Diversity & Inclusion* about benchmarking and measurements. But before I wrap up this chapter, I want to mention a bit about these management tools and how they apply to your D&I success.

D&I SCORECARDS

There are **dashboards and *D&I Scorecards*** available for reference and application to your annual assessment of diversity and inclusion within your organization. But the best tools are developed by and for your own Association, because you have established your own goals, and that is the core around which your measurements are based.

As a framework, you want to consider the following four strategic areas of your organization's business, and design ways to assess your goals and progress within each one:

- Workforce
- Workplace
- Community
- Marketplace

I will go over each one and what your targets are in these four areas. As part of my *Big Six Strategies for Success,* I have identified **six steps to develop a scorecard.** The idea is to apply them all to each of your four benchmark or dashboard areas.

The six guiding steps are as follows:

1. Identify what your Association accomplished last year, where it's headed next year, and what budget is needed in order to accomplish these two things: do a

thorough measurement; and realize the pre-identified *diversity objectives.*

2. Use this scorecard to establish a baseline. It will tell you, as CSE, along with your Board and other governance exactly where the organization is, at the moment. It points out areas for improvement and change. Embellish this scorecard so that it includes specific, defined, and measurable D&I goals. Also identify what person or department will be responsible (i.e. held accountable) for each aspect.

3. List those annual goals as developed from the baseline, and then define strategies for making change. This is a very helpful planning activity to do each year-end.

4. Because management accountability is essential for your D&I strategy to succeed, some Associations link diversity goals and objectives to cash bonuses or incentive programs in order to enhance the buy-in of their leadership.

5. Detail your workforce levels. Assemble information on the demographics of your Association's executives, board members, volunteers, and staff.
6. Check both your goals and baselines to see that they meet regulations and compliance requirements (e.g., EEO, Affirmative Action).

So, in a bit more detail, let me define these four action areas for your scorecards.

A. WORKFORCE: This is "Who We Are"

You measure your workforce as part of your management of Association talent. You want to identify and quantify your diverse target populations, and compare them with the numbers of non-minority men. You should be able to enumerate this diverse talent breakdown in each of the following aspects of your Association:

- Recruitment
- Hiring representation
- Movement--both promotions and lateral

- Retention versus attrition and turnover
- Talent assessments, leadership development, and competency gaps
- Corporate engagement

B. WORKPLACE: This measures "How we Work Together"

The key purpose of a D&I strategy is to build an inclusive culture within your organization that will attract and retain diverse talent, supporting and encouraging them to thrive internally and advance your mission externally.

There are numerous fascinating and informative studies on workforce and workplace satisfaction, many done and presented by Gallup and Quantum Workforce. They offer tools for polling or canvasing your Association to identify how your managers, staff and volunteers feel vis á vis your stated inclusion goals. This will help you know the status quo, and develop your own definitions for progress.

Gallup talks about "satisfiers" and "dis-satisfiers" for employees of organizations, regardless of demographics. You can find them at Gallup online or in my D&I book's chapter on benchmarking. But the summary is that the higher number of "satisfiers" your team identifies within your Association workplace, the better their output or performance is going to be. These "satisfiers" really do link to results, so they are useful elements of your benchmarking of the workplace.

Polling isn't the only way to evaluate the levels of engagement of your workforce. Some Associations use one-on-one meetings or town hall meetings and focus groups. The idea is to let your various populations be heard, and to gather feedback about the ways D&I are working or could be improved. It is important that every employee of whatever rank or background is asked the same set of questions. This will give you the best data for analysis.

C. COMMUNITY: This is "Where you Serve"

Each of your D&I goals and initiatives can be used to develop metrics or measurements around the benefits you bring to your community.

You can count how many diverse community organizations you partner with, for example, and who is represented in their constituencies. You can enumerate the "impressions" that your Association makes in touching diverse stakeholders, both physically and in social media. You can count the number of scholarships you give, internships you offer, or services that impact your diverse community segments. It is also helpful to encourage your Board of Directors and staff members to be more involved in community organizations or events, and then to figure out how those efforts and exposure can be measured. You can also assess levels of awareness of your diversity message throughout the community.

Design, support and encourage outreach opportunities for every level of talent at your Association. Then try to quantify the specific Return on Investment of your diversity initiatives. Can these results be leveraged in order to encourage retention of your staff or customers? Or enhance your image?

D. MARKETPLACE: This is "Who You Serve"

The deep idea behind your Big Six Strategy for D&I success is that D&I is good business. You should be able to discern and plan for concrete impact on your marketplace from any and all D&I goals and initiatives.

Start by developing benchmarks that define diversity goals for your programs, mission success, client and constituent acquisition and retention. Map these against your target groups. Notice how you can use this data in fundraising efforts by making them part of the story you tell in grant applications and funding requests.

Other marketplace elements that you can measure are the demographics of program or event participants, and the supplier diversity attached to your vendors and venues. You should be able to see concretely how D&I is manifest in your spending and program statistics.

All four of these strategic areas are important to your D&I strategy measurements. Numbers are powerful. They can inspire, they can tell great stories, they can influence your Board and annual budget planning, even your broader strategic planning and institutional direction. I encourage you to use D&I metrics as tools to support your efforts and enhance your success with all of your Association stakeholders because they are very helpful in getting others to join you in making important diversity changes within your organization.

D&I is the New Normal for non-profit and for-profit corporations. As an Association Executive, your charge is to ensure that D&I becomes a key business strategy for your organization. The framework presented here is a proven strategy, one that you can follow to ensure success, generate an accurate review of your diversity status, inspire discussion, planning, and implementation, and then make it happen in a meaningful way.

CHAPTER 14

NEW-SCHOOL LEADERSHIP FOR THE 21st CENTURY

There are many fascinating books available that offer insight into leadership, including some on the CAE Authoritative Literature List. I wrote *New-School Leadership: Making a Difference in the 21st Century* because I found that many of these authors were not making clear that the needs for and demands on leadership have changed radically in the past few years. To be a dynamic and effective leader of an organization or corporation today requires an entirely different strategy and set of skills than it did just five or ten years ago. In fact, much of the best advice and examples from even the last decade *no longer apply.*

My book grew out of my own implementation of best leadership practices in my professional life as Chief Diversity & Inclusion Officer for the United States Tennis Association. It springs from a widely-shared definition of effective new-school leaders by scholar and leadership-studies pioneer Warren Bennis that they are "those who innovate, originate, initiate, develop, focus on people, inspire trust, have a long-range view, ask what and why, have their eye on the horizon, and challenge the status quo."[5]

In this chapter, I want to offer a summary of what I determined to be the fundamental ways to become and remain the most effective leader possible given the current institutional and corporate landscape. My hope, with this introduction as with the full book, is to ensure that we have inspiring and visionary leaders at the heads of our organizations, divisions, and institutions.

I have distilled my vision for a new-school leadership model into the following components:

L = Lifelong Learner
E = Engagement
A = Ahead of the Curve
D = Diversity & Inclusion
E = Empathy
R = Relationship Management
S = Social Media Presence
H = High Energy
I = Influence & Enrollment
P = Platinum Rule

I am convinced that these are what constitute a skilled, successful, and happy leader of any sort of business today: corporation, association, or organization; it applies to leadership in the for-profit, government, educational and NGO sectors, as well. Given the dynamic and progressive environment that we all face as leaders of Associations, I believe that we need to focus on those tenets in order to improve and solidify our leadership capacity. I go into the components of this model in depth in my book, but I want to introduce you to the model in this chapter. To these I add a core group of "must-have" attributes which ensure that a 21st-century leader makes the impact to which she or he aspires in our swiftly-changing world. The "must-haves" are:

- **Vision**
- **Purpose**
- **Passion**
- **Good Communication Skills**
- **Management Ability**

There are many ways to apply this model to your own enterprise in order to gain the "unfair advantage" that we all seek to dominate our sector or sphere. I'll introduce you to a few of those ideas here, as well.

As Holly Green, CEO and Managing Director of The Human Factor, Inc., summarizes so concisely in her *Forbes* blog, "Previous generations of leaders could at least count on a reasonably stable world, where change unfolded at a much slower pace. These days, the past is increasingly less predictive, the future is almost unimaginable, and the present exists for about a nano-second."[6] Where once we looked to our leaders to administrate and direct, we now require them to guide and inspire. Effective leaders in volatile times need vibrant visions that "cut through today's clutter of information to communicate (them) to multiple stakeholders in a memorable way."[7]

The transformation that is required by this radical shift ripples through every aspect of our business life.

The major characteristics of highly successful leadership in the past involved the "top-down" model of an authoritarian approach to running companies or organizations. Strict protocols and regulations accompanied precise orders by professional managers. Once a leader took a decision or direction, he or she then enlisted his or her managers to do *what* was wanted by prescribing *where* and *how* it was to be done, and *when* it needed to be accomplished.

Traditionally, problems were solved by blaming and shaming. Many firms tended to look outward from the inside, with a sole priority of making the maximum profit for shareholders without regard for the unique needs of their customers. In addition, employees were often tired, bored, stressed, and unsatisfied.

It's been said that old-school organizations were perfectly well designed to obtain the results that they achieved. So if our leaders and their organizations maintain any aspects of that traditional strategy, they are destined to produce the very same things. Today, however, we need <u>new</u> results in order to keep up with the more connected world in which we find ourselves.[8] **Success** in any and every sector that you can name already means something altogether different.

New models of leadership for attracting stakeholders, for training staff, and for organizing institutions now have to meet the realities of today, and the challenges of tomorrow. Everything is different now, including how we lead!

Today's management landscape is complex. Our employees span multiple generations, cultures, and backgrounds; they have very different styles, interests, and needs, not all of which are compatible with one another! Our marketplaces are highly competitive, expectations are high, loyalty is fleeting, and customer attraction and retention is very different than it once was.

In fact, you could say that there really is no longer a conventional "manager" environment at all. "Today's employees want to be led. They want to participate and engage in every aspect of their job."[9] This is exciting, actually, when you're a leader. The opportunities are ripe for development and success. But they now demand a much more participatory style of leadership, and consistent two-way channels of communication, in order to succeed.

This mode of leadership has become critical in part because, "in general, people do not like to have ideas or solutions imposed on them."[10] New-school leadership skills involve inspiring and engaging followers without mandating or ordering. What has become critical to the effectiveness of leaders today is to achieve a concrete, participatory "buy-in" from everyone involved in a decision, direction, or departure.

My **10-part leadership model** identifies the critical components of a new-school leader. Each aspect can be cultivated and practiced as a way of making us more successful and satisfied in our pursuit of leading great organizations and corporations.

L = Lifelong Learner

Every great leader today is curious and committed to the constant pursuit of new knowledge, skills, and understanding. Many leaders have terrific educations, and/or are mentored by the best, in their rise to the top of their Associations or business entities. But there is no end to the available wisdom about psychology and human nature that we can study and absorb, information about developments in technology and communication that we need to keep abreast of, and the inspiration that can be drawn from success stories around us, not to mention the perceptive insights that can be gleaned from our employees, our customers, our kids, and all of the other stakeholders of our enterprise.

What makes **lifelong learning** a top component of new-school leadership is the starkly apparent fact that virtually no occupation or industry remains the same over time, any longer. So not only does each job need to be updated and learned, but so does the holistic comprehension of leaders who lead employees that perform those jobs.[11]

I also support the idea of **pervasive learning** that Dan Pontefract describes in his book *Flat Army,* about "learning at the speed of need,"[12] and how it is impossible for a leader to "know" everything about a subject anymore, but that she is totally capable of knowing where to find critical information on any topic, when the need arises.[13] The other component of **pervasive learning** is that we have now done away with the idea of "training as an event," which is a fixed, closed-end mindset; the new-school leader replaces that with, as Pontrefact summarizes it, "learning (as) a collaborative, continuous, connected and community-based" growth mindset.

Furthermore, I believe that new-school leaders should expect continuous learning and self-improvement "from every person at every level of (your) organization."[14]

E = Engagement

New-school leaders make engagement a top priority. As best-selling author Peter Economy (*Managing for Dummies, The Management Bible, Leading through Uncertainty)* reminds us, "Every employee is a source of unlimited ideas on how to improve his or her organization's products, work processes, and systems. Most employees simply need to be invited to participate and then positively reinforced when they do."[15] Mr. Economy adds this critical rejoinder, however: "employee participation only works in an environment of complete and unconditional trust."[16]

That is where new-school leadership in the area of **employee engagement** comes in. Excellent leaders commit time and resources to inspiring engagement, setting engagement standards and benchmarks, and measuring their progress in institutions large and small.

A = Ahead of the Curve

Since one of the core responsibilities of any leader is to lead change, and since change is not just a given within marketplaces and companies today but is happening at break-neck speed, the new-school leader makes it a priority to remain **ahead of the curve.** Part of the **life-long learning** effort of successful leaders is to stay attuned to evolving trends. Their leadership vision and implementation must involve planning for and adapting to those social, technological, and economic developments that directly impact their corporation and stakeholders, or that *may* do so, in the very near future.[17]

New-school leaders must remain in a position to observe the directions and consequences of trends both on the ground and at a macro-level (and everywhere in between, of course!). They need to be able to synthesize input from many sources, whether it is through employees or clients, online or at home, in networking groups or about competitors, and then stay open to a flexible, swift adjustment of their strategies and response. New-school leaders who stay ahead of the curve are nimble, and they build their organizations in such a way that everyone can respond to trends.

D = Diversity & Inclusion

Obviously I've discussed this at length in the previous chapter. I believe that most savvy executives today already are attuned to the diversity of the contemporary U.S. marketplace, the New Normal. However, I was surprised to learn that a recent comprehensive global leadership survey shows that while leaders of diverse organizations do value this component of leadership and corporate strategy somewhat, nevertheless, "leaders worldwide rank diversity of lowest importance among all leadership zones."[18] This is a grave mistake.

Every new-school leader needs two things: a full understanding of the diverse make-up of the full complement of their stakeholders and potential clients; and a comprehensive **diversity & inclusion business strategy** that builds not just their company, but its profit and influence, going forward.

E = Empathy

Jet Blue Airways Chairman Joel Peterson lectures at the Stanford GSB, and is known to remind young entrepreneurs and future leaders that "You catch more flies with honey." This is not new news, but his students are well aware that some schools of management still encourage leaders to "set a high bar and withhold praise, or to motivate by fear."[19]

Those who ascribe more to Peterson's approach cultivate **empathy** in their new-school leadership, and attune themselves emotionally to the psychological experiences of others. They lead with their hearts open to the needs and lives of those around them.

We must be very cognizant of ways to expand our consciousness when leading others in the 21st century. To begin with, a new-school leader's commitment to D&I invariably helps him or her to be exposed to and then embrace others' views and approaches.

From this vantage of expanded understanding of the myriad perspectives in a leader's personal and professional landscape, accompanied by a genuine interest in and concern for the circumstances of those around her, a leader can begin any action or negotiation from a place of cooperation and compromise. "By accepting the concept that we can all learn from each other, we can start to understand how to turn personality differences into positive business results."[20]

Empathy is a part of the new-school leadership model that needs particular attention because psychological research trends show many ways that the power that accompanies leadership can specifically diminish many varieties of empathy.

R = Relationship Management

The new-school leader's business, like her or his personal life, depends on other people, both for its profitability as well as for the impact of its services or products. Time and again it has been shown that a person's ability to build equitable relationships is directly related to their effectiveness in business. So, excellent leadership demands that both thought and effort be put into **forging strong, rich relationships** on all fronts: clients and customers, colleagues and peers, distributors and suppliers, co-workers and employees, boards of directors and service providers, community leaders and competitors.[21]

The building and management of a new-school leader's relationships involves forthright and excellent communication, which are skills that I discuss in depth in later sections, too. We mentioned already that *dialogue* rather than mandates, *empathic listening*, and an *openness* to information and input from all levels of a leader's professional and personal life are part of the ideal and critical new-school communication strategies. As Peter Economy (*Managing for Dummies, The Management Bible*) reiterates, "the best leaders encourage an open flow of ideas throughout the organization, and break down the walls that separate employees from one another."[22] This is the foundation of excellent relationships.

New-school leaders start by identifying and establishing those very best and specific high-quality relationships that will deliver on their mission. They also know how to cultivate and grow strong relationships by learning first about the needs of each party. Relationship management also involves the negotiation of power struggles that leaders often encounter within their high-test management teams.

New generations of workers have a different relationship to their companies and work life in general, so they will have a different relationship to leadership. They have observed in their parents' experiences the ways in which work-related burnout generally lowers quality of life, and they have noticed the lack of loyalty that companies demonstrated towards Baby Boomer workers over the last twenty years. As a result, workers and leaders aged 22-46 are defining a different relationship to how they earn a living, including telecommuting, continual training for professional evolution, and flexible hours. They aren't impressed by the idea that a job is something that you hate, or that you're "paying your requisite dues" through professional suffering and tough, dull work. These are not things that they value or tolerate well.

They know how to be more efficient through technology and they don't look to leaders or managers to supervise progress too closely. Their relationships are very much grounded in the teamwork model and they invest a great deal in collegial relationships. They do respond to feedback, but they are looking at leadership and management structures generally more as a "lattice" than in terms of the long-familiar corporate "ladder."[23] New-school leaders manage their workplace relationships by enmeshing with their employees and by appreciating the priorities and feedback of their multi-generational team members.

S = Social Media Presence

New-school leaders know how to harness the potential in social media as a way to realize their vision. They maximize social media tools in order to build their personal and corporate brands, in conjunction with their Association's image, and they use these platforms to support their two-way communication and relationship management with staff, customers, markets, stakeholders, and future or potential communities.

Social media covers a spectrum of online sites, applications, and services. New-school leaders cultivate their presence in professional areas like LinkedIn, as well as on interactive platforms like Twitter. They know, for themselves and for their companies, projects, or programs, that Facebook is more than a place to share family anecdotes, and that Google+, Pinterest and Instagram can be easy ways to build and expand select networks.

As Duke Adjunct Business Professor Dorie Clark wrote in the *Harvard Business Review*, "If your digital footprint is lacking and you don't have a presence on basic sites like LinkedIn or Twitter, you're likely to be dismissed as a *Luddite*. Indeed, even the basic notion of writing a resume is becoming antiquated; your 'shadow resume' is Google."[24] New-school leaders are very savvy about being sure that their profiles are consistent, positive, and reflect well on themselves and their enterprises. They keep their information current, but don't overexpose themselves on multiple sites or pages.

H = High Energy

The energy of new-school leaders is noted by everyone who they encounter, from customers and stakeholders to staff and employees to informal community members and new contacts. Their energy is compelling to follow, and it communicates the leader's willingness to pursue a vision vigorously, even in spite of pre-existing rules or outmoded systems. New-school leaders embrace a very high energy in order to deliver on their ambitions with a fearless and unique single-mindedness.[25]

Of course, with high energy comes high awareness: new-school leaders are always cognizant of the big picture, the total landscape, and they use their capacity to hold all that they see in balance. Stanford GSB Professor Robert Sutton has noted how research shows that high-energy leaders, those who accomplish a great deal, "have high positive <u>and</u> high negative affect, which means they're really optimistic and confident things will turn out in the end, *but* they're really, really worried about every little detail and how it's going to screw things up."[26]

High-energy leaders are also able to increase their efficiency through leveraging technology. This temperament matches the newest generation of colleagues and staff.

I = Influence & Enrollment

It is not a new-school leader's *power position* that accomplishes what she wants done: it is her ability to *influence* people—both inside and outside of her association or institution—that determines her ultimate success. This begins by getting others to *enroll, trust, and respect* in her vision and integrity. Other tenets of leadership support her ability to influence, as well, including empathy for and appreciation of other points of view and cultures, along with deliberate communication which brings those views and communities to her project or purpose.

Enrollment occurs only after it is clear that a leader has recognized the potential impact of a decision or request on stakeholders or populations who may have very different values and priorities than her own. She will often employ her attention to diversity and inclusion, and the wisdom that she gleans from her D&I plan, in order to maximize enrollment in her vision.

This has become all the more important as new-school leaders' businesses and customers have become more global. New-school leaders do need to remain mindful and intentional about the influence they wield and the values to which they ask their myriad stakeholders to subscribe. Loyalty and respect are *earned* by new-school leaders, and not automatically expected. Talent pools and stakeholders are influenced by the openness, transparency and clarity of communication offered by those leaders whom they seek to follow.

P = Platinum Rule

New-school leaders are much more attuned to the *Platinum Rule* than to the Golden Rule. The latter is certainly familiar, as it's also called the "ethic of reciprocity": to treat others as you would like them to treat you; concomitantly, this means <u>not</u> treating others in ways that you would <u>not</u> like to be treated (sometimes called the Silver Rule). Sliding up the list of precious metals, writers Tony Alessandra and Michael J. O'Connor have done the primary work of outlining the now popular Platinum Rule. It has grown in importance for new-school leaders because not everyone is *like* us, so <u>they</u> *don't want* to be treated the way <u>we</u> do!

Put most simply: the Platinum Rule recommends that we treat others the way _they want_ to be treated.[27] Like other qualities in the new-school leadership model, including those of empathy and inclusion, the Platinum Rule encourages leaders to remain keenly attuned to the styles and feelings of others as distinct from their own, and to respect those styles and feelings as having their own integrity and priority. As Alessandra explains it, "the focus of relationships shifts from 'this is what I want, so I'll give everyone the same thing' to 'let me first understand what they want and then I'll give it to them.'"[28]

The reason that I include this in my model is not just to update a common aphorism, but because the Platinum Rule looks at ways for new-school leaders to have productive relationships. It advocates treating people in ways that they appreciate, and encourages leaders to use language with employees and colleagues to which they relate.

In addition to this leadership framework, there are **five foundational must-haves** for any future leader.

MUST-HAVE—VISION

The way that new-school leaders realize change is not just by *managing* it: they *cause* it. And they begin by articulating a vision for the future, something that they believe in and are compelled to push into reality. Vision is a leader's "new picture of the future," and the organizing principle around which goals are set and plans are made.[29]

Many organizations and managers outline a **vision statement** for their enterprise which describes, in words, "where and what an organization wants to be in the future."[30] This document is a standard component of institutional structure, but is not the same as a new-school leader's **vision.** Vision is about action, a compelling picture that is generated in the imagination of a new-school leader that inspires forward motion once it is shared with clarity and passion.

Vision is absolutely essential to new-school leadership because, without it, a leader's staff and stakeholders are bound to lose focus and pursue inefficient actions or directions.

MUST-HAVE—PURPOSE: Why

If **vision** is the idea of where a leader's association or organization is going, then **purpose** is **why** we follow that leader there. A new-school leader must concentrate on communicating their vision for each stakeholder in an enterprise, but, even better than the explanation, they also position everyone's work "as part of a larger big-story purpose." Xerox PARC guru John Seely Brown describes it this way: "The job of leadership today is not just to make money. It's to make meaning."[31]

In part, our motivations for work and change are shifting in the 21st century. We are less enchanted with work for work's sake, or doing dull tasks long-term for purely financial reasons. Even though everyone wants and needs appropriate compensation and benefits, and even when we are able to negotiate a balance between work and personal life, still, more than ever, we want to know **_why_** we are undertaking our endeavors. So new-school leaders really examine the purpose for their own vision, the reason behind their mission, and the "why" for each project and strategic direction. Where the answers are connected to a higher good or a transformational contribution to community and planet, leaders find their message to followers all that more compelling.

MUST-HAVE—PASSION

Passion shows that we care. It is something in our demeanor and expression that can clearly be seen: by our boards and our customers, by our teams and our stakeholders. It is a clear signal of our deep belief that we are doing important work which can bring about positive change, and it is an energy that inspires others to follow us in action and deed.[32]

Passion does not succeed in a vacuum. As Oracle CEO Mark Hurd reminds us, passion is but one component of new-school leadership. The "fiery and high-energy" expression of vision and personality must always be accompanied by hiring great people in the best positions to execute any "breakthrough strategy" that a leader designs and communicates about through their position.[33] Passion doesn't stand alone, but it is a powerful new-school leadership attribute, and an essential component for moving people and organizations towards change.

While part of being a new-school leader is believing passionately in the purpose or "why" of your vision,[34] equally important is your passion for those you work with and for. Starbucks CEO Howard Schultz uses the word "passion" in interviews frequently, and not about coffee! His passion is for "treating his employees with dignity and respect," because "happy employees lead to happy customers."[35] Sir Richard Branson, founder and CEO of the Virgin Group, also expresses in interviews his passionate commitment to everyone on his team, so that they can "elevate customer service."[36]

MUST-HAVE—GOOD COMMUNICATION SKILLS

Compelling visions must be communicated, clearly and with passion, in order to create the change that a new-school leader desires. One of the communication challenges that we all face these days is all of the competing information, inputs, distractions, and data that swirl around our listeners, wherever they may be. As new-school leaders undertake to develop their top-notch communication skills, one of their major priorities is to share their vision in ways that are memorable, and that stand out from all the other ideas and inputs that bombard their teams constantly.[37]

Excellent communication skills dovetail with a leader's engagement and commitment to diversity and inclusion as well, of course, because communication is a dialogue by which they interact and share with team members and stakeholders across the full spectrum of their organization or enterprise. In a global marketplace with a multi-cultural workforce and client base, new-school leaders must constantly evolve new ways of communicating—that is, on a two-way basis—as well as connecting through emerging technologies and platforms. One key priority of excellent communication skills in any leader is to ensure consistency, but new-school leaders also must deliver their message in ways that are compelling to each level and background of their various stakeholders and team members, so that organizations and companies are motivated to take the right action in the very best way.[38]

MUST-HAVE—MANAGEMENT SKILLS

New-school leadership requires solid skills for managing others and for understanding the role and responsibilities of those managers who make up the executive ranks of their association, organization, or corporation. Leadership is not management but, that said, **leaders do nothing alone.** New-school leaders understand that essential management skills—the "order and consistency (of) drawing up formal plans, designing organization structures, and monitoring results against the plans,"[39]—are necessary to deliver on their ambitions.

Leaders establish the direction that their companies will take by starting with their concrete vision for a distinct and vibrant future. They then undertake an interactive development process with their management team members and stakeholders in order to plot their course of action. Through the techniques, skills, and strategies that I have outlined thus far, they build alignment and enrollment by communicating their vision, along with the "why"—the reasons for following them; they inspire their teams to persevere together through challenges.

Leaders need to ensure that their projects are managed appropriately by people who think flexibly, creatively, and independently[40], even if managing directly is not something that they do themselves. "A leader is ultimately measured by his/her effectiveness, and because of that, the team surrounding them must be equipped and managed to support the goals of that leader."[41]

Excellent management skills are the key to executing a leader's vision and strategy. New-school leaders need to "drive operational excellence," as Oracle CEO Mark Hurd summarizes it. And this attention to operations is what "brings the strategy alive with dynamic new products, sales teams that are highly intelligent and engaging, and brilliant new talent that sees the company as a terrific destination."[42]

~~~~~

My longer book also goes into the ways in which new-school leaders can apply this framework to gaining what I call the "unfair advantage" in any market sector or business. This involves leveraging digital and social media, an understanding of trends, their ability to handle change, personal likeability and great listening skill to their maximum ability, and in service of their mission and their organization. I encourage you to read it!

CHAPTER 15

STUDY STRATEGIES

I found the recommended reading to be the most helpful part of my preparation for a successful CAE examination. We all study differently, and best retain information in different formats and to varying degrees. The material that relates most directly to your executive duties and orientation will be the easiest to review, so establish a schedule that introduces you to the newer or less familiar concepts and subject domains first.

Work backwards from your designated test date and identify the three months that you can dedicate to learning and review for your CAE exam. Lay out a day or weekend to cover each book or each chapter related to the domain you are reviewing, and figure that you'll also need a few weeks after reading to re-read and refresh your memory on what you have covered. Make a schedule, put it in writing, and keep to it in order to minimize stress and cramming.

Anticipate a minimum one week for learning and study on each domain. For this designated reading/study period, you may need to drop something from your daily schedule in order to establish regular, concrete study time. Highlighting works for many students; others work better taking notes for later review. Create flashcards as you read, particularly around the key concepts and defined terms here and in your other books.

I have presented a few mnemonics here, but build some of your own to remember key groupings. In the reading, look for "scenarios" or potential situations for a CSE to address, within each of the books on association management best practices. You will be asked to think as a CSE throughout the test, but the challenge is to apply that to scenarios beyond your current professional association or position.

Consider forming or joining a study group with other CAE candidates who are not in your association. As I mentioned in the domain about education programs, adult learning is different than that of a younger student, so recognize that discussion and conversations will help to solidify your facility with various concepts and information. Organize discussions and review of the domain concepts within your group, on a scheduled formal basis, and have one or two study group members present each domain or subcategory.

Open a DropBox or wiki to share information, articles, and documents together that can supplement your reading and review. If a regular physical meeting is not practical where you live, organize a conference call or Skype group meeting. Consider inviting key local leaders as guest speakers on issues, like one association's CFO, or another's Of-Counsel non-profit attorney, to supplement the CAE candidate's "teaching" of various issues and subject areas.

If you can't participate in a study group, do schedule lunches or meet-ups with other non-profit leaders or board members, just to get their perspectives on the material that you are studying. Your own association leaders and colleagues can be very supportive and helpful, particularly those that deal with content of their own. Ask them for some time off to study, too!

In each area of review, consider where there may be commonly held misconceptions, or practices and approaches that are "the way you do it," but which may not be the most current or innovative approach to a situation or strategy. The ASAE has selected the recommended reading in order to encourage CAE candidates to familiarize themselves with the "generally accepted best practice" in association management. That means that the practice is legal, found in **research-based literature or scholarly writing,** not necessarily restricted to non-profits, adapted from **current business literature** but also "tried and true in the association management field," and recognized by the ASAE and The Center in its various publications.

The ASAE also provides workbooks with practice tests and sample scenarios that are well worth incorporating into your examination preparation. There are also test-taking tips and practice exams available at ASAE's knowledge center at www.asaecenter.org/collaborate. (You do need to be an ASAE member preparing for the exam to access the site.) Learning how to dissect each question is a skill that you must include in your test preparation process.

As I suggested above, approach each question by reading it slowly without guessing either what it's asking or what the response should be. Circle the "qualified words," like "not," "first step," and "best practice," as they are pointing you to a correct and incorrect answer. If there are irrelevant details within the question, cross them out first, so they don't distract from your deliberation. Do identify the parties involved in each situation, and their relationship to one another; this will assist in selecting the correct governance or management response.

Next, determine whether this question pertains to one of the processes discussed in this study guide, like SPIE, RFP, and LERP. Do these or others of your mnemonics help? After these steps, re-read the question. It should be simpler, now; decoded. Eliminate the two wrong answers that have either nothing to do with the situation, or have an obvious flaw, like an illegality, or incorrect time frame or process. Then, re-read the question and subject the two remaining answers to the following questions: Is it a Best Practice? Is it legal, ethical, reasonable-relational and practical-procedural? Does it fit the question's stated time constraint? Does it reflect a decision that should be made by the CSE, not a board or other staff member? One answer should be "best overall," if not perfect.

As you begin taking practice exams—and don't dive into those until you have done your initial learning of the subject matter in all nine domains—

research the answers you miss, go back and highlight in your notes those areas where you have made mistakes, and research best practices for any subjects where you are not yet able to consistently determine the correct response. In the later stages of review, focus your study sessions on the notes and key word flashcards you have made for each domain, plus the highlighted corrections information.

Remember that you need to complete your application and qualification materials at least three months prior to your test date, so schedule your preparation and submission concurrent with your initial exam prep time. The experience and course/educational requirements must be complete at the time of your submission, and you'll need to include all of the documents that prove your eligibility.

CHAPTER 16

THE CAE TEST DAY

As of this writing, the CAE examinations are still given on the first Friday in December, and the first Friday in April. They are always given in cities with major association hubs, like Chicago, New York and Washington, D.C., and the other test cites rotate around additional locations. Once you know your date and research the locales, if you are more than 120 miles away or there is a small group of test takers in your area, contact the ASAE to see if they can assist you in traveling, or can set up a test closer to your home base.

Be certain that you arrive rested and relaxed for your test day. Remember to plan for a good night sleep on the two nights prior to the examination, even if it involves travel to your test destination. Testing begins at 9 AM, so schedule your arrival 30-60 minutes before that. It runs for four hours. You'll receive an email six weeks before test dates that you must return in order to register for the exam. Then, within 10 days of the registration deadline, you'll receive a second email that confirms your exam date and location.

When you check in, you will find your name on the roster. Bring your membership number (if you're a member), a photo ID and bottled water, but no books, papers, food, coffee, or PDAs. You'll be expected to sign a confidentiality agreement, and will be warned that any copying or disclosure of test materials is punishable by law.

There are 200 questions, but you can take your time on every question. Read each one carefully: don't jump to some conclusion about what it asks. There should be triggers in the question or scenario phrasing. Rule out the two clearly incorrect responses right away. Do a SPIE analysis for procedural questions, and LERP on policy situations, always remaining in the mindset of a Chief Staff Executive during every scenario presented for your response. Come back to best practices whenever possible: these are the tent poles of your study and subject organization.

Use your question deconstruction strategy delineated in the study section above. Answers are not necessarily "correct," because the CAE exam is designed as "practice-based," not "citation-based." You are looking to select the best option by using your judgment and decision-making capabilities.

Additional mindsets to remember are that questions will pertain to federal law not state law, and anti-trust liabilities are always of paramount importance in association management. Board deals with board matters; staff deals with staff. What may appear to be a public relations issue regarding volunteer to volunteer or staff to staff may in fact pertain to governance. Answers are often research-based, so make that a first step for planning marketing, media, and other strategies.

Keep Best Practices in mind: that is the thinking behind the test's creation: "best business practices, best human resource practices, best accounting practices, best public relations practices, best governance practices, best meeting planning practices, best education practices, best volunteer management practices." These are the key concepts you have gleaned from all of your reading, study, and sample testing. Bring them with you, on exam day.

CHAPTER 17

SUMMARY & CONCLUSION

I hope that you reach this point in my book with a great deal of enthusiasm and forward momentum towards tackling the CAE application and examination process. Whether you are just considering the prep process, or already have your studies underway and your test date on your radar, you have still taken the essential first steps towards achieving an attainable and valuable goal. I won't pretend that this accreditation process isn't hard work. But I do believe firmly that it is rewarding and worthwhile.

Like any professional certification—the law bar exam or the medical boards, for example—the CAE test does require solid study and time-consuming review. The good news is, like those other challenging evaluations, it always draws in part on the best practices and practical experiences of your current position as a senior association executive. So the areas where you need to do most reading, networking and review are those very same ones that you don't happen to encounter in your job every day, already. This offers you a chance to expand in fascinating ways.

I think that you'll find it interesting to learn about some of these additional aspects of non-profit management, and can often use your pursuit of these additional subject areas to meet new colleagues at other associations or professionals at different firms who can fill in your knowledge gaps while becoming part of your professional cohort. I hope that you'll deepen your personal awareness of D&I as a strategic decision for your Association through this study, and I encourage you to dive into my additional information on new-school leadership when you have time!

I know that the experience of reading this book and working through its topics, new and old, will enhance your Association Management skills no matter what your next steps. I hope that you will share your insights with me, as did the readers of my first edition.

This book is best used as a resource in tandem with the ASAE's recommended book list. If you find yourself at the beginning of your journey to CAE exam day, follow its many recommendations for supplemental reading, study group development, and self-testing. Chart your preparation on a calendar, and build in vacation and celebration points. Plus, as I suggested earlier, add some additional padding for the inevitable detours and crises that come up in our jobs.

Once your exam day is over and your results are in, be sure to reward yourself. You will have achieved an important and highly respected accomplishment. I look forward to congratulating you!

D.A. ABRAMS

REFERENCES & RESOURCES

- <u>Diversity & Inclusion: Big Six Strategies for Success</u>, D.A. Abrams, 2013
- <u>New-School Leadership: Making a Difference in the 21st Century</u>, D.A. Abrams, 2014
- *7 Measures of Success: What Remarkable Associations Do That Others Don't*, American Society of Association Executives, 2012
- *Professional Practices in Association Management: The Essential Resource for Effective Management of Nonprofit Organizations,* 2nd Edition, by John B. Cox
- *Core Competencies in Association Professional Development*, by Terri Tracey, CAE, and Kathleen M. Edwards, CAE, 2011
- *The Will to Govern Well: Knowledge, Trust & Nimbleness,* 2nd Edition, by Glenn H. Tecker,

Paul D. Meyer, Bud Crouch, and Leigh Wintz, CAE, 2010

- *Association Law Handbook*, 5th edition, by Jerald A. Jacobs, 2012
- *How to Read Nonprofit Financial Statements*, 2nd Edition, by Andrew S. Lang and Wayne Berson, 2010
- *Creating and Managing an Association Government Relations Program*, 2nd Edition, by Amy Showalter
- *Membership Essentials: Recruitment, Retention, Roles, Responsibilities, and Resources*, by Sheri Jacobs, CAE, and Carylann Assante, CAE
- *How Are Your Ethics?* by Jennifer Baker and Janice Dahl, 2009
- *Human Resources Policies and Procedures for Nonprofit Organizations* by Carol Barbeito, 2004
- *Nonprofit Marketing Best Practices* by John Burnett, 2007

- *The Volunteer Management Handbook*, 2nd edition, edited by Tracy Connors, 2012
- *The Jossey-Bass Handbook of Nonprofit Leadership and Management*, 3rd edition, by Robert D. Herman, 2010
- *Leading for Innovation: And Organizing for Results*, edited by Frances Hesselbein, Marshall Goldsmith, and Iain Somerville, 2002
- *Millennium Membership: How to Attract and Keep Members in the New Marketplace* by Mark Levin, 2000
- *The Power of Partnership: Principles and Practices for Creating Strategic Relationships Among Nonprofit Groups, For-Profit Organizations, and Government Entities* by the Plexus Consulting Group, 2008
- *CAE Study Guide*, ASAE and Knapp & Associates International, Inc., 2010 (new edition due early 2015)

ABOUT THE AUTHOR

Author—Speaker—Leadership Advisor—D&I Expert—Association Management Expert

D.A. Abrams has been involved in tennis since he was introduced to the sport through the National Junior Tennis and Learning (NJTL) of Philadelphia. As a junior player he excelled in the sport, earning national rankings in the United States Tennis Association and the American Tennis Association. Good grades along with hard work on the tennis court earned Abrams a tennis scholarship to attend Millersville University of Pennsylvania. After graduation, he put his accounting degree to good use at Control Data Corporation based in Minneapolis, Minnesota.

Missing tennis, Abrams returned to Philadelphia after four years in the Twin Cities to serve as the Recruitment Director and Head Tennis Professional at the Arthur Ashe Youth Tennis Center (AATYC). While at AAYTC, he launched Dave Abrams Tennis Services, a full service tennis company offering tennis instruction to adults and juniors as well as International Tennis Tours. Abrams has been a certified member of the United States Professional Tennis Association and Professional Tennis Registry since the early 1990s.

In 1993, Abrams moved to White Plains, New York to join the United States Tennis Association

(USTA). Currently he serves as the Chief Diversity & Inclusion Officer. He has also served in the following capacities: Executive Director of two USTA Sections (Eastern, 2006-2012) and (Missouri Valley, 1997-2000); Director of Community Outreach (2000-2006); and National Coordinator, NJTL & Minority Participation (1993-1996).

Abrams also serves as a volunteer for the following: American Society of Association Executives (ASAE)—Diversity & Inclusion Committee; The Conference Board—Council of U.S. Diversity & Inclusion Executives; University of Arkansas—Walton College of Business—Office of Diversity & Inclusion Advisory Board; World Golf Foundation—Diversity Advisory Council; and Mount Sinai—Center for Multicultural & Community Affairs Advisory Board.

As a board member of the Alzheimer's Association—Hudson/Rockland/Westchester, New York Chapter (July 2009 to June 2013), Abrams served in the following roles: Chair, Audit Committee; Member, Compensation Committee;

Member, Nominating Committee; and Member, Development Committee. In addition, he played an active role in the New York Society of Association Executives—NYSAE (2010-2011) as a member of the Membership Committee, and Education Committee. It should be noted that Abrams is a Certified Association Executive (CAE).

Abrams believes in life-long learning and loves to read. He also loves to write, and is the author of _New-School Leadership: Making a Difference in the 21st Century_; _Diversity & Inclusion: The Big Six Formula for Success_, as well as *Association Management Excellence: Becoming an Expert by Preparing for the CAE Exam*. All books are available in print, digital, and audio wherever best-selling titles are sold.

Abrams enjoys travelling with his wife Shelia D. Abrams, and has travelled to all of the states within the United States with the exception of four. Countries that he has visited outside of the U.S. include: Australia, Morocco, Barbuda, Antigua, Denmark, Sweden, Norway, England, France, Italy,

China, Thailand, Brazil, Costa Rica, Jamaica, Mexico, Canada, Spain, Indonesia, and the Bahamas.

Over the years, Abrams has made many media appearances. Featured appearances include: "America's Black Forum" hosted by James Brown to discuss the mission of the USTA's Community Outreach department; participated in a Satellite Media Tour (15 Markets across the United States) with tennis legend Zina Garrison to discuss African Americans in tennis and the National Junior Tennis & Learning Network; and CNBC's *Rivera Live* as a panelist to discuss the impact of Venus and Serena Williams on tennis participation among multicultural groups.

Recent print articles include: *Exec of the Future: D.A. Abrams—Different Strokes* (http://associationsnow.com/2012/09/exec-of-the-future-different-strokes/); and *Serving Up Diversity: The USTA's D.A. Abrams—Diversity Executive* (http://diversity-executive.com/articles/view/serving-up-diversity-the-u-s-tennis-association-s-d-a-abrams).

Connect with D.A. on Twitter: @DAAbrams1

Instagram: www.instagram.com/DAAbrams1

LinkedIn: D.A. Abrams, CAE, *www.linkedin.com/pub/d-a-**abrams**-cae/7/a04/459*)

Facebook: David Anthony Abrams, www.facebook.com/david.a.abrams.1

INDEX

10-part leadership model.................. 237
501-c-3.................... 103
501-c-4.................... 103
80-20 rule 97
990EZ....................... 36
abandonment matrix assessment 152
Abstract and information management systems 91
accrual basis............. 30
Active Listening 53
Activity ratio............. 32
Ad Hoc committees 111
ADDIE 170
Advocacy 121
affiliation agreement 115
Affinity Programs.. 165

alignment of goals and values 217
allocation rule......... 125
alternative gross-up method................ 126
Andragogy 168
annual audit............. 32
annual fund 155
anti-trust violations. 78
Articles of Incorporation 110
association 102
Association image . 211
association reserves 30
audit committee 112
balance sheet 33
balanced mode 104
Banquet Event Order (BEO).................. 159
Benchmarking 95
Benefits, marketing 175

best practices for governance 106
best practices for sponsorships and partnerships 217
Blended learning... 168
Board of Directors 106
Branding 27, 176
build trust 50
business continuity planning 84
business plan 87
Bylaws 110
capital budget 37
capital campaign....156
capital expenditures 38
capital gains 33
Cash........................ 34
cash-basis................. 30
cause-related marketing...........179
C-Corp.................... 104
chart of accounts..... 30
charter agreements 116
Chief Staff Executive 106
civil liability..............81
Clayton Act.............. 79

clean audit 32
Coalition building ..131
code of ethics......... 146
co-employment 71
Collaborations 23
Collaborative win/win 59
Combined Cash & Accrual Statement 30
communications.... 172
communications channels............. 184
communities of practice 92
community relations 181
compensation surveys 95
compliance program 78
Component relations 115
compressed time 71
confidentiality 86
conflict of interest ...86
Conglomerate or combination associations 105

consensus model ... 109
consent agenda 109
Constructive Confrontation 50
contingent organizations 105
contract 65
contracts 160
copyright 80
corporate and governance documents 79
coverage ratio 32
credentialing program 161
Credentialing programs, 4 types 162
criminal liability 81
crisis communications and management plan 185
CSE termination 67
cultural audit 220
current ratio 31
D&I Scorecards 221
data 90

Directors & Officers liability insurance 82
disabled person 73
Distance education 168
diversity 200
Diversity 57
diversity statement 204
due diligence 81
efficiency ratio 32
eight core Knowledge Management tasks 92
Endowments 156
environmental scan 173
Environmental Scan 45
environmental scanning 46
equal opportunity employer 72
estimation rule 125
ethics program 145
Evaluation 170
Executive committee 106
Exempt employees .. 71
expenditure test 123
explicit knowledge .. 90

external influences, marketing 174
external relations .. 120
external research 94
facilities management 83
factors essential to solid internal controls 40
Factors in staff recruitment 63
features 175
Federal Election Committee (FEC) 130
federation 104
Financial key indicators 29
financial projections 28
five foundational must-haves 253
flexibility 47
flextime 71
fluidity 46
Formative evaluations 95
for-profit subsidiary 41

Four Ps of Marketing 173
fundamental theories 24
global association .. 144
globalization strategy 144
golden handcuffs 141
Government relations 119
gross up method 126
growth objectives 43
High impact Boards 108
Human Resources ... 61
Inclusion 201
Individual cash contributions limits 127
industry relations .. 182
information 90
information of competitive value 190
Informed intuition .. 55
innovation 199
insurance coverage. 80

-277-

integrated publications program............ 186
intellectual property80
Internal research..... 94
international association.......... 144
international strategic alliance 143
Invasion of privacy 189
issues management132
Job descriptions...... 74
Knowledge management .89, 90
LAI Principles of Fundraising....... 154
leadership competencies........51
Leadership through data.........................51
Legal and Risk Management....... 77
LERP 63
lifelong learning....238
Liquidity ratio 31
Lobbying 122
logical project management processes 24

maintenance objectives............43
management letter ..35
market analysis 95
marketing plan 176
maximize volunteer capacity................54
media advisory 184
media relations...... 181
member relations .. 134
member research.....96
membership categories 137
membership classes 137
Membership dues structure 137
membership section 137
Mentoring................58
message framing ...180
methods of reporting 98
Needs Analysis of your audience..............140
New media............. 191
nimbleness...............47

no substantial part test 123
Non-exempt employees 70
Non-lobbying activities 122
numerical summaries 97
Omnibus Budget Reconciliation of 1993 125
One-to-One marketing 177
open information 36
open space meeting 161
operating budget 37
operating ratios 95
operational plan 87
organizational culture 51
organizational success can be blocked 25
organizational uncertainties 25
OSHA's General Duty Clause 83
Overhead 37
Pareto Principle 97

patents 81
Pedagogy 168
performance management 67
performance review process 66
permanently restricted net assets 33
Permission marketing 178
personal liability 82
Personnel files 65
Planned giving 156
political action committee (PAC) 126
press conference 184
press release 184
Primary research 94
privacy policy 136
productivity 199
Professional associations or societies 102
Professional Development Programs and Delivery Systems 166

profit/loss statement 34
Profitability ratio 31
program development 151
Promotion 181
proxy tax................ 125
public affairs 181
Public Policy........... 119
public relations 135, 172
quality control 97
quota sampling 97
ratio method........... 126
reasonable accommodation... 73
Reasonable membership restrictions 138
reasons to form 41
Reciprocal or Unified associations 105
research agenda 92, 93
resolving conflicts .. 117
response models 46
retention................. 199
retention calls......... 175

Robinson-Patman Act 79
Sarbanes-Oxley 39, 112
S-Corp.................... 104
Secondary research .94
section 273a method 126
segregation of duties 39
Self-regulation programs............ 146
Sexual harassment .. 67
Sherman Act 79
six steps to develop a scorecard............ 221
social media........... 180
Special events 155
Special interest groups 113
staff reductions....... 68
Staff reductions legal checklist.............. 68
staff-driven 103
Standard-setting Programs 147
standing committees 111

statement of activities 33
statement of cash flows 34
statement of financial position 33
statement of revenue and expenses 34
strategic partnerships 216
Strategic Program Budgeting 37
strategic public relations program 179
stratified sampling.. 97
succession plan 26
Succession planning 115
summative evaluation 95
supplier diversity ...213
tacit knowledge 90
Talent optimization 209
target audience for diversity............. 206
Target marketing ...178

Task Force 111
taxable functions 36
Technology administration..... 75
technology plan 76
temporarily restricted net assets 33
termination 69
the ADA 72
the Federal Trade Commission Act .. 79
three-tiered association......... 105
Trade associations. 102
trade secrets 81
trademarks 80
traditional media... 192
Transparency......... 106
Two-tiered associations 105
UBIT 35
Ultra Vires 82
Undue hardship 73
unqualified audit..... 34
unrestricted funds... 33
value proposition ...175
values 44

vendor and supplier management 85
vision 44, 253
Visioning 43
volunteer leadership development 115
volunteer-driven.... 103
website development strategy 190

ENDNOTES

[1] Visconti, Luke. "Ask the White Guy: Why White Men Must Attend Diversity Training." www.diversityinc.com.

[2] Bush, Vanessa K., "The Cultural Connection." http://diversitywoman.com. 23 January 2011.

[3] Dougherty, Conor and Jordan, Miriam. "Minority Births Are New Majority." *Wall Street Journal.* 17 May 2012.

[4] U.S. Census Bureau, 2010.

[5] DiMattia, Ernie. "Leadership vs. Management," quoting Warren Bennis, *On Becoming a Leader*. New York: Basic Books, 2009.

[6] Green, Holly. "Leadership: Then and Now." *www.Forbes.com*. 30 Aug 2011.

7 Stephenson, Carol, O.C. "How Leadership Has Changed." *Ivey Business Journal/From The Dean*. July-August 2011.

8 Cole, Neil. "Old v. New Leadership: A Study in Contrasts."

9 Green, Holly. "Leadership: Then and Now." *www.Forbes.com*. 30 Aug 2011.

10 The Evolution of Leadership." *MindResources Institute of Learning and Innovation*. Vol 2, Issue 2, pp 1-9.

11 Green, Holly. "Leadership: Then and Now." *www.Forbes.com*. 30 Aug 2011.

12 Pontrefact, Dan. *Flat Army: Creating a Connected and Engaged Organization*. Wiley: New York, March 2013.

13 McKinney, Michael. "Leading Views: Pervasive Learning." www.leadershipnow.com/leadingblog. 15 Jan 2014.

14 Ash, Katie. "Building a District Culture to Foster Innovation." *Education Week Magazine*. 2 Oct 2013.

15 Economy, Peter. "7 Ways to Lead With Your Heart." *www.inc.com*. 14 Feb 2014.

16 *Ibid*.

17 "The Evolution of Leadership." *MindResources Institute of Learning and Innovation*. Vol 2, Issue 2, pp 1-9.

[18] AchieveGlobal with Craig Perrin, Sharon Daniels et al. *Developing the 21st Century Leader*. Tampa, Florida: AchieveGlobal World Headquarters, 2010.

[19] Dunn, Andy and Ekiel, Erika Brown. "Passion is a Prerequisite." 11 Dec 2013. *www.gsb.stanford.edu/news*.

[20] "Building Better Business Relationships." *www.businessblogshub.com*. 6 Dec 2013.

[21] "Building Better Business Relationships." *www.businessblogshub.com*. 6 Dec 2013.

[22] Economy, Peter. "7 Ways to Lead With Your Heart." *www.inc.com*. 14 Feb 2014.

[23] "Leadership by the New Generation: Bridging the Age Gap." *www.mindtools.com*. MindTools.com. (Year). Article/Resource Title. [Online]. Available from: http://www.mindtools.com/full-URL. [Accessed: Date].

[24] Clark, Dorie. "How to Reinvent Yourself After 50." *HarvardBusinessReviewNetwork*. 13 Dec 2013.

[25] Demartini, John. "On Inspired Leaders." *Business Brief Magazine/* bbrief.co.za.

[26] Sutton, Robert and Rao, Hayagreeva. "How do You Scale Excellence." *www.gsb.stanford.edu/news*. 7 Jan 2014.

[27] Alessandra, Tony and O'Connor, Michael. "The Platinum Rule: Discover the Four Basic Business Personalities and How They Can Lead You to Success." New York: Warner Business Books, 1998.

28 Alessadria, Tony. "The Platinum Rule." *www.platinumrule.com/aboutpr.asp*

29 Callahan, Clinton. "Becoming a Leader to Change the World for the Better." *www.radicalhonesty.com*. 26 Nov 2013.

30 Zmorenski, Debbie. "Why Leaders Must Have Vision." *www.reliableplant.com*. 29 Jan 2009.

31 Economy, Peter. "7 Ways to Lead With Your Heart." *www.inc.com*. 14 Feb 2014.

32 Tredgold, Gordon. "10 Things You Can Do to Improve Your Leadership Today." *www.leadership-principles.com*. 13 Feb 2014.

33 Hurd, Mark V. "Five Leadership Qualities Great Executives Must Have." *www.linkedin.com/post*. 9 Dec 2013.

34 Greenberg, Melanie. "Six Qualities Leaders Need to be Successful." *Psychology Today*. April 2012.

35 Gallo, Carmine. "Seven Ways to Inspire Employees to Love Their Job." *Forbes.com*. 21 June 2013.

36 Gallo, Carmine. "Seven Ways to Inspire Employees to Love Their Job." *Forbes.com*. 21 June 2013.

37 Stephenson, Carol, O.C. "How Leadership Has Changed." *Ivey Business Journal/From The Dean*. July-August 2011.

38 Zmorenski, Debbie. "Why Leaders Must Have Vision." *www.reliableplant.com*. 29 Jan 2009.

[39] "Can you Turn Someone On Your Team Into a Good Leader?" *www.businessblogshub.com*. 1 Oct 2013.

[40] Denning, Steve. "The Key Missing Ingredient In Leadership Today." *www.Forbes.com*. 27 July 2012.

[41] MacDonald, Matthew. "Leadership–Influencing Through Relationship." *BusinessBlogsHub.com*. May 2011.

[42] Hurd, Mark V. "Five Leadership Qualities Great Executives Must Have." *www.linkedin.com/post*. 9 Dec 2013.

www.ingramcontent.com/pod-product-compliance
Lightning Source LLC
Chambersburg PA
CBHW030307080526
44584CB00012B/472